The Power Behind Positive Thinking

The Power Behind Positive Thinking

Unlocking Your Spiritual Potential

Eric Fellman

HarperSanFrancisco
An Imprint of HarperCollins*Publishers*

Grateful acknowledgment is made for permission to quote from the following works: From *Parade* magazine, quotes from Rene Russo. Copyright © 1995. From *Zinger* by Paul Azinger with Ken Abraham. Reprinted with permission from *Guideposts Magazine*. Copyright © 1995 by Guideposts, Carmel, NY 10512.

HarperCollins Web Site: http://www.harpercollins.com

FIRST EDITION

Library of Congress Cataloging-in-Publication Data
Fellman, Eric.
The power behind positive thinking : unlocking your spiritual potential /
Eric Fellman. — 1st ed.
Includes bibliographical references.
ISBN 0–06–062315–2 (cloth)
ISBN 0–06–062316–0 (pbk.)
1. Success—Religious aspects—Christianity. I. Title.
BV4598.3.F45 1996
248.4—dc20 96–20399

96 97 98 99 00 ❖RRDH 10 9 8 7 6 5 4 3 2 1

For Joy,

who first taught me

to believe in Faith, Hope,

and most important, Love.

Contents

Acknowledgments

Like most books, I imagine, this one was not the product of only one person. I wish to thank, first and most important, Dr. Norman Vincent Peale and Mrs. Ruth Stafford Peale. Dr. Peale patiently taught me about myself and life in such a way that opened up a new universe of meaning for the word *faith*. Mrs. Peale, by her leadership and example, has shown the world how to take an idea and transform it into practical programs that work.

Then there are the people of North Scituate Baptist Church in Rhode Island and their pastor, Ted Pitt, who first sat through a series of talks on these ideas nine years ago and still encouraged me to write them down in a book. Pat DeMatteo of International Center for Creative Thinking got tired of hearing me talk about writing a book and set my first deadline by saying, "Either write that book or quit talking about it." Trent Price took the manuscript under his wing as an agent and found Harper San Francisco where Senior Editor Patricia Klein gave me the high praise of "promising" as a first-time writer and then proceeded to help me re-shape the manuscript through hours of phone calls and hundreds of yellow sticky notes. John Allen gave patient editorial guidance that saved me much embarrassment and saved the reader from confusion. Wendell Forbes gave invaluable counsel.

All of these friends and others who read and commented on parts of this book did so for you, the reader. May you find help here to build your life into a pattern that makes sense and opens your spirit to the wonderful power behind positive thinking.

The Power Behind Positive Thinking

Introduction

It was my privilege to work for Dr. Norman Vincent Peale during the last nine years of his life. In that time he wrote six of his forty-two books, gave hundreds of speeches, and set the course for the future of the Peale Center for Christian Living. It was important to him that the center stand for telling what he called "the whole story of positive thinking."

His most famous book started with the words, "Believe in yourself! Have faith in your abilities! Without a humble but reasonable confidence in your own powers you cannot be successful or happy."

That book, *The Power of Positive Thinking,* which has been translated into forty-one languages, has sold more than twenty-five million copies worldwide. More important, the philosophy of positive thinking appears everywhere: in sports, entertainment, politics, sales meetings, and parenting seminars. It's truly a concept that has circled the globe.

Through the years many people have copied and expanded on Dr. Peale's techniques, often leaving his spiritual emphasis out of their work. But Dr. Peale was convinced, and he convinced me, that no amount of self-belief, self-talk, attitude adjustment, or other technique can be of lasting benefit unless a person understands and maximizes the spiritual element that stands behind the technique.

The Power of Positive Thinking is filled with references to the connection between spirituality and the development of true personal power. Following the dramatic statement that opens the first chapter of that book—the words quoted above—Dr. Peale states, "Put yourself in God's hands. To do that simply state, 'I am in God's hands.' Then believe you are *now* receiving all the power you need."

When I first went to work for Dr. Peale, I asked him to promise to pour a little of himself into me during my tenure with him so that I could learn enough to give out the message to others. Over the years there were several such "pouring" occasions, and I discovered that my life and beliefs were profoundly affected by them. This book is my attempt to tell of that transformation and to share some of what I have learned (so far) in a way that I hope will be helpful to my generation.

You'll find nine simple concepts in this book, arranged in three sets of three concepts each. The root of all nine ideas can be found in the writings of Dr. Peale, but what's said in this book is my interpretation of those ideas. I wouldn't presume to tell you what he thought; all of his books are still available, and you can read them to discern his views yourself. However, I've attempted in these pages to share how what I learned through Dr. Peale's work has shaped and molded my thinking, enabling me to approach the most important things in life in a fresh and helpful way.

Here, then, are the nine concepts, beginning with the first triad:

Cornerstones

Simplicity
Inner Quality
Divinity

These cornerstone concepts describe principles that are universally true for all human development.

The second triad—qualities that are born into all of us, from which we can build a strong inner self—then builds on those cornerstones:

Foundations

Belief
Optimism
Kindness

Finally, building on those foundations, the following framework pieces give a structure that sustains our physical, mental, and emotional life:

Framework

Faith
Hope
Love

As a tool to help readers move through this book, I've described these nine concepts as providing the basic building materials for a simple three-dimensional pyramid. The image of the pyramid reveals the simplicity, strength, unity, and symmetry that underlie a balanced and happy life.

Throughout the book I offer practical suggestions for the application of each concept, examining and highlighting each through stories of how real people—people like you and me—have used them to great effect. As you read, I trust you'll discover that I'm describing a journey we're taking together. Our roles are like the "night hikes" I used to take with my brother in the Minnesota woods of our boyhood years. One of us would go ahead several dozen yards and then shine the flashlight back along the trail; the other could then see the rocks, roots, and bushes and move forward at a steady pace. I'll try to pick a careful path and shine the light into places you need to see in hopes that together we can travel a fair distance.

PART ONE

Assembling the Materials for a Basic Life Pyramid

In this first section we'll outline the basic elements of the life pyramid concept. We'll define those basic qualities we all possess through which we can shape our lives. Those elements are the cornerstones, foundations, and framework pieces of a life structure that can be built from materials you were born with. Once constructed, the life structure you build will be unique to you and will provide the support you need to strengthen your physical, mental, and emotional being.

No metaphor (including this pyramid concept) is perfect. What is important about a metaphor is that it provides a basis for understanding deeper truths and a handle we can grasp to take hold of those truths in our own lives. The pyramid concept has done that for me, and I hope it will for you. Because I've learned many of life's most important lessons in a canoe, canoeing is another metaphor I rely on; it helps me understand and remember those life lessons. Let me share one such lesson before we start.

One summer during college I got a job leading wilderness canoe trips with high school young people. We would leave the Minneapolis area on a Sunday afternoon and head north to the Boundary Waters Canoe Area in Voyageurs National Park in northern Minnesota. Returning on Friday afternoon, I would spend Saturday washing clothes and buying supplies for the trip leaving the next day.

One of the trips later in the summer involved a group of guys, ten of us altogether, two in each canoe. Having successfully led three or four trips already, I was feeling pretty confident. We decided on a more difficult route that included some mild white water. Arriving at the head of the first rapids, I dropped off my passenger and instructed the others to tie up on shore while I investigated the "line" we would have to find to successfully negotiate the fast water.

Poised in the quiet swirl just above the downward sweep of the river, I decided the line was easy and swung my canoe into the fast water without any further preparation. This was not a good idea, for I had a canoe full of supplies, including most of our food.

Halfway down, trouble came up fast. Attempting to thread my way between two boulders, I overcorrected. With no one to help, I was soon washing sideways down the rushing stream. The inevitable happened: the canoe became wedged between two rocks and blocked the water coming behind. The river then did what any sensible river will do: it washed over this puny temporary dam, taking me and all the supplies with it.

Fortunately I was wearing my life vest and had the presence of mind to grab the food box, which as a result filled only halfway with water before I splashed up on shore. Once the laughing and taunting stopped, the other guys helped me collect the canoe and those bits of gear that we could find. But I had learned a valuable life lesson: always unload your baggage before negotiating fast water.

Working on your inner life is like shooting the rapids. It takes preparation, a few good techniques, diligent effort, and single-minded focus. As we begin this journey together, I encourage you to unload any baggage you're carrying. Perhaps you've tried to gain life focus in the past and not been successful. Maybe you're carrying religious baggage that interferes with exploring your personal spirituality. Whatever your baggage, set it on the shore for now and come with me for an exhilarating ride into new discoveries. You can always come back later along the footpath and pick up any important items you need for the rest of your journey.

Chapter 1

Cornerstones

On a very warm July day in 1992, Dr. Norman Vincent Peale's secretary appeared at the door of my office and said, "Dr. Peale is outside in his car. He'd like you to come out for a few minutes."

I went to the side door of the building, and sure enough, there he was in the front passenger seat of his 1984 Cadillac Sedan DeVille with a yellow legal pad perched on his knee. He motioned for me to open the driver-side door and said, "Climb in for a minute, Eric. Mrs. Peale and I are headed for New York today. She went upstairs to get some mail and make a phone call, but I decided to stay here where it's cool."

Holding up the yellow pad, he continued: "I've begun thinking about another book, and I wanted to bounce some of the opening ideas off you."

Pause with me a moment and catch a glimpse of the wonder of this encounter. In July 1992 Dr. Peale was one of America's most admired people. Besides his famous best-seller *The Power of Positive Thinking*, he had written forty other books during a fifty-year span. They had sold more than twenty-five million copies in forty-one languages across one hundred and twenty countries. Now, at ninety-four, he was working on his next book!

Glancing down at the pad, he said, "This will be a book for this country I love so much. Because America seems to be drifting, I want to write about what's needed today."

"What do you have so far?" I asked.

"Well, the first thing is more faith; that's the most important. Then I'd like to write about commitment, discuss sacrifice, and maybe reexamine the power of prayer. I realize that these are highly spiritual subjects, but I believe Americans are more open to spiritual subjects today than they were twenty or thirty years ago. How do you feel?"

For the next twenty minutes I listened in wonder as Dr. Peale described the concepts for his book, asking occasionally for my feedback. When we finished, he handed me a page of notes for his secretary. On that page he had indicated topics and ideas he wanted researched in the current media and in his own vast file of articles, speeches, and sermons. This was the beginning of his last book, which he titled *In God We Trust.*

That was also the beginning of this book. Hearing that the deepest and most important truths that shape our lives and our nation are spiritual truths, I was challenged by Dr. Peale's driving passion at ninety-four years old. Soon after, I began jotting notes, ideas, and diagrams, which became the basis of this book.

We live in the age of science, when everyone seems to be from Missouri, the "show me" state. Credence is given only to material that can be held, felt, smelled, touched, or heard. This approach can be grossly out of touch with reality, however, for the most important forces in the universe are not matter, but spirit.

Why does one sports team win against incredible odds? The winners point to their never-quit spirit, and the losers claim, "We just didn't want it badly enough." You'll hear about a similar phenomenon if you ask any doctor whether she or he has ever had a case that seemed hopeless except for the patient's will to live and the force of prayer. Interview the top thousand CEOs of worldwide corporations, and they'll say that the keys to success are vision, mission, and attitude—in short, inner values of the spirit.

Yet for all of this affirmation, why do we spend so little time and money discovering and maximizing our spiritual potential? Billions of dollars are spent annually on diets and exercise equipment by people trying to lose weight. However, any doctor will tell you that weight loss begins with the attitude and mental focus of the person, not with pills, powders, or calorie counts.

The failure to pursue spiritual potential in this country is grounded in the unique American confusion of the word *spiritual* with the word *religious*. Because our nation was founded by Pilgrims seeking freedom to exercise religion without governmental restraint, we've erected careful walls around our public institutions to keep religious influence from flowing in and to keep influence over religion from flowing out. In no other country in the world—not even Communist nations—is this wall so impenetrable. In fact, in England, the home from which the Pilgrims fled, high school children are required to study religion in its generic sense in order to be informed of its place in the forces that affect our world.

But *religion* is not *spirituality*. Simply defined, spirituality concerns matters of the spirit; it describes the inevitable search all human beings undertake to answer their questions about a Supreme Being or Higher Power. My word for this being is *God*, and to simplify this book, that's the word I'll use. But use any word that's comfortable for you, because we're talking about your personal spirituality, not religion.

Religion, on the other hand, is any person-made system that defines a particular method of conducting that search. Spirituality is based on our innate longing, while religion is based on rules and regulations set out to define (and sometimes control) that longing.

Let me illustrate this distinction with a story that shows how ridiculous we've become in trying to divide our lives. I was recently asked by the local guidance counselor to speak to the combined high schools of a northern Ohio school district on the topic "Make Positive Thinking Work for You" as part of their Career Focus Day. The program's sponsors wanted the students to look to the future with optimism and excitement.

This was no easy assignment, for keeping the attention of today's teenagers is a formidable task. On top of that, the planners of the day, without my knowledge, had decided to divide one thousand students into two equal groups and had asked me to fill not one but two eighty-minute sessions.

With only forty minutes left before the first session, I was sitting quietly in the school library trying to compose my thoughts and figure out how to fill eighty minutes without totally losing my audience. Echoing in my mind were the words of advice that my sixteen-year-old son had given me as I left home for the trip. Knowing I had some anxiety as I prepared to speak to a group of his peers, he tried to reassure me. Gripping my shoulder, he said, "You'll do fine, Dad. Just don't make a fool of yourself!"

Some comfort.

About ten minutes before my session was to begin, a man rushed in and identified himself as the superintendent of schools. He seemed extremely agitated and was holding a piece of paper that was trembling in his hands.

"You're a minister, aren't you?" he asked anxiously.

"No, not really," I replied.

"Now wait a minute," he insisted. "I have your résumé right here, and it says you're an ordained minister."

"It's true I went to seminary and have been ordained," I said, "but I don't serve in a local church. My full-time job is being head of the Peale Center, and I'm here in that capacity today. I'm well aware that my talk is to be about positive thinking, not religion."

"Oh, that's a relief," he said. "I got concerned when the guidance counselor handed this to me and I saw that you were ordained. As you know, this is a public school, and we can't talk about God here."

"Just a minute," I replied. "I said I knew the talk wasn't to be about religion, but I didn't say anything about God. A discussion about God can be about personal spirituality, not religion."

With that, an anguished look came over the superintendent's face, and he grew flushed. "Please try to understand my position. I may agree with your personal views, and we may even attend similar churches. But you can't talk about God in a public school. If you insist on doing so, I'll have to ask you to stop your presentation. That would ruin our Career Focus Day, and we don't want that, do we?"

I could see it was no time for an argument about the difference between spirituality and religion, so I smiled warmly, put out my hand, and said, "Please don't worry. I'm here today to try to help the students gain hope and confidence for their future, not to create an uncomfortable situation for you by debating the separation of church and state."

We shook hands and walked to the auditorium for the first session. Sitting on the platform waiting to be introduced, I watched the students stream into the room—noisy, friendly, eager. Most of them were probably just happy to be out of classes for the day, but the look of anticipation on their faces grabbed my heart. More than anything else in that moment, I wanted to offer a presentation that would help them make the most of their potential and find a full and satisfying life.

Then I noticed the superintendent standing along the back wall with several other adults (members of the school board, I later found out). His arms were folded rigidly, and his face still wore a look of concern. Maybe if he had relaxed and shown trust, what happened next wouldn't have occurred. Who knows? (But it sure was fun!)

After the introductions were completed, I glanced to my right and saw the solution to my dilemma. Standing before the students, I said, "My son, who's a sophomore, warned me not to make a fool of myself this morning. However, at the risk of doing so, I must tell you that a grave concern has been expressed over my presentation today. Why don't you all turn around and look at the folks along the back wall. They're all really worried that I'll do something wrong and use the G word today. How about helping me out? Everyone please stand."

With groans, the clatter of books dropping to the floor, and the clack of theater seats folding up, five hundred students rose from their seats. Turning to my right, I said, "Please repeat after me . . ."

Slipping my right hand over my heart, I looked at the American flag and began, "I pledge allegiance to the flag of the United States of America, and to the Republic for which it stands, one nation under God . . ."

Stopping and waving my hands at the crowd, I shouted, "Wait a minute, wait a minute! Say that again!"

Noticing the puzzled looks on their faces, I repeated the crucial phrase, "One nation under God," and waited while the wording registered.

"What was that again?" I then asked the gathering.

By now the students had caught on and were laughing gleefully. They roared at the top of their voices, "One nation UNDER GOD, indivisible, with liberty and justice for all!"

"Okay, sit down," I said. "Now does anybody have a dollar bill?"

A big African-American student wearing a football jacket waved a bill over his head. "Stand up, young man," I said, "and read us what's written just above the word *one* on the back of that dollar."

For just a second he looked puzzled; then a grin broke over his face and he read, "In God we trust."

"What was that?" I asked.

"IN GOD WE TRUST," he boomed.

When the laughter subsided, I glanced at the back of the room and saw sheepish grins, so I continued. "All of you students had better watch out, for you've just repeatedly used the G word and may be liable for suspension.

"Now that we've had our laugh, though, let me make a simple point. You've just recited the pledge of allegiance to our country—a statement in which the fathers of our nation saw fit to highlight the need for a spiritual focus. You're here today to consider what it means to get a job and have a career. In many ways the dollar bill is a symbol of everything that's right about America, a symbol that explains why we're the nation to which many of the immigrants in the world long to come. Only in America can you start out with just one of those bills in your pocket and, with hard work, create a whole pile of them—enough to own your own home, car, and television and send your children to college, all in one lifetime. In many other parts of the world it takes generations to own a home or send a child to college.

"A dollar bill has no worth by itself, however. It represents trust in our nation to continue to prosper. And our nation believes that the ability to prosper has spiritual roots: 'In God we trust.' We believe it so much we print it right on every coin and every bill of every amount.

"So if I come here today to talk to you about how to get a successful start in life, I have to tell the truth. Success starts from the inside out. Part of building yourself up on the inside is dealing with your spiritual life. What you think about God, how you relate to God, and how you address the spiritual concepts of Faith, Hope, and Love affect your choices of career and family.

"All I'll say to you today is that just as it's okay to carry around a dollar bill and say the pledge of allegiance in school, it's okay to think about God in school. It would be wrong for me to do anything to impose my set of beliefs on you. I happen to be a Protestant minister, but we aren't going to talk about that. We're just going to get you to think about the energy and strength you can draw from personal spiritual exploration. Of course, if any of you want to ask me about my beliefs once we get out to the parking lot, I'll be happy to tell you about them."

A chuckle rose from the crowd—a chuckle that even put a grin on the superintendent's face. The rest of my talk went smoothly, although I'm not sure about the results with the students. The biggest response I got was from a group of girls who came up afterward and wanted to know if I carried around a picture of my son!

But I did make a connection with the superintendent. He came forward smiling and said, "Pretty smart trick, Reverend, but you'll have to pull the same stunt with the next group to get off to such a good start."

"Well," I said, "you'll have to help out by standing in the back again and pretending to frown!"

The power behind positive thinking is a power from your spirit, a spiritual power. How you focus and formalize your spiritual power becomes your religion, but that's another subject—a subject that it's not essential for you to address before beginning the process of finding within yourself the incredible resources available to anyone who wants to unlock the potential we all have to become what we want to be. As you read this book, I'm sure my religious views will peek out from behind some words and phrases. They've become such a part of my life that it would be impossible for me to hide them completely. So let's get a few things said here at the outset. The phrase that best describes my religious orientation is "Christ-follower." I've dedicated my life to fully comprehending and living by the example and teachings of the historical person Jesus Christ, who I believe lived, taught, was killed, and was resurrected almost two thousand years ago in the ancient land of Palestine.

But please understand the earlier-mentioned difference between religion and spirituality. Open yourself to spiritual exploration and growth and ignore any phrases I use that set your religious antennae tingling. If you want to talk religion, see me afterward in the parking lot.

Which brings me to another important point before we tackle the main issues. This book is for beginners, people like me who are just starting to understand the presence and power of the spiritual in their lives. Perhaps even people who are skeptical about spiritual matters but are willing to come forward with an open mind, to begin a seeking process.

If you're mature spiritually, this book may seem like baby food to you, bland and tasteless. If your religion is well defined and you're highly committed to it, you won't be satisfied with the questions I leave open for later discussion. That's fine; just give the book to a hurting or seeking friend who doesn't yet have your confidence and commitment and let it help that person get started.

Our discussion of this system of personal growth, and the development of our spiritual potential, can be greatly helped through the use of a simple model. I would like us to think of a three-dimensional triangular pyramid. Such a pyramid has three equal triangles for sides and a fourth triangle resting on the ground, as shown in the following diagram.

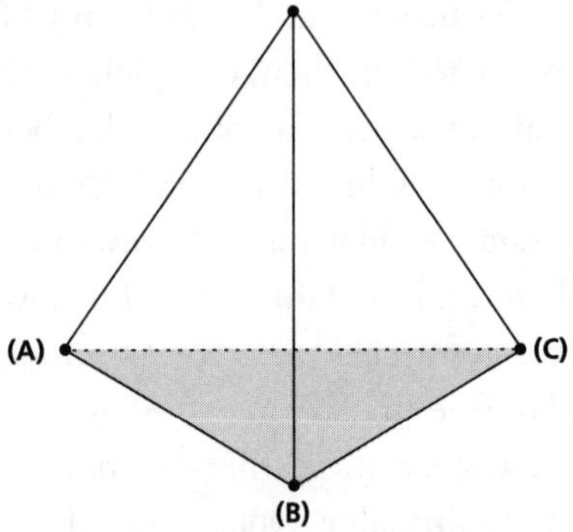

In this model the cornerstones of the foundation are points A, B, and C. As we build our model, let's begin with the "ground floor"—the horizontal triangle—and work with these cornerstones.

I call the cornerstones of the foundation of a life that taps into spiritual potential Simplicity, Inner Quality, and Divinity. Let's look at each in turn.

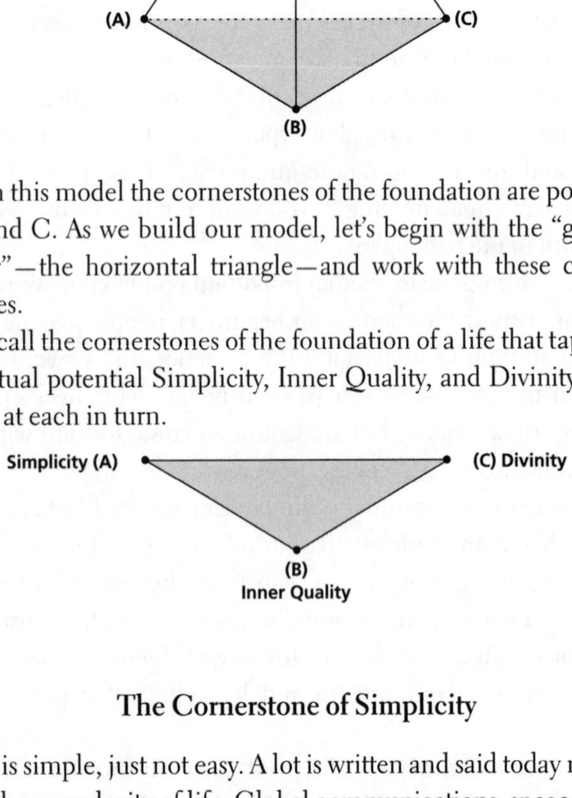

The Cornerstone of Simplicity

Life is simple, just not easy. A lot is written and said today regarding the complexity of life. Global communications, space travel, and computer information systems are all supposed to be so bewilderingly complex as to render the average citizen nearly helpless to cope with the modern world. The solution? Believe the pundits, and you'll think you must surround yourself with cadre of experts. Get a nutrition consultant to eat right, a mutual fund adviser for investments, a tax adviser for tax matters, a mentor for your business, and a trainer for your exercise program.

Any of these people can help you in a single area of your life, but if you're looking for personal fulfillment, none of them will ever get you closer to your goal. Only *you* can do that. Personal fulfillment requires recognizing what's important in life and choosing to take action yourself.

Think of it this way. If I want to bench-press two hundred pounds, the task is very simple, although it certainly isn't easy. It's been twenty years since I lifted weights regularly, but I imagine my limit now is under one hundred pounds. If I wanted to lift two hundred pounds, I'd have to start at seventy-five and work up through a regular plan of lifting that would take me several weeks or months.

Let me put it another way. Circumstances in the world have changed a lot in the last hundred years. Cars, computers, airplanes; the rise and fall of Hitler, Soviet Communism, and disco music. But people don't change. The Michael Milkens of the world still shock us with their greed even as Mother Teresa amazes us with her selfless love. One mother gives her life holding her baby above the rising waters of a Midwestern flood while another straps her helpless children into a car and drowns them. I can fly off the handle at my wife, Joy, when she chides me about the twenty pounds I've gained and yet tremble in fear over the possibility of losing her when she's twenty minutes late driving home through an ice storm.

The essentials of life are very simple. Look for that simplicity and work on those essentials by your own choice and effort, and the results you want can be yours. Stop looking for a magic formula behind every infomercial and self-help book, including this one. Realize what they offer: *self-help*. This book and the many other good ones in the field are tools for you to use, not miracle cures to be passively received.

The wisdom of a simple approach is found in the most famous book of ancient wisdom, the Bible. Speaking to some rather pompous adults, Jesus said in Matthew 18:3, "Unless you change and become like little children, you will never enter the kingdom of heaven." The meaning? Spiritual principles are simple, although they're not always easy to follow.

This book will be simple. When you get through, you'll know three foundational principles, understand three structural principles, and have three kinds of tools to use to build the structure upon the foundation. You'll also go through a section that talks about applying the foundational principles, structural principles, and tools to every aspect of your life—to the triad of physical, mental, and emotional being.

Remember, simple doesn't mean easy. Lifting two hundred pounds takes work, but that work is work easy to understand, to set goals for, and to build toward through the habits of accomplishment.

The Cornerstone of Inner Quality

The second cornerstone of the pyramid is the concept of Inner Quality. The simple proverb, "You can't tell a book by its cover," speaks to this principle. Only what's inside, often hidden from view, determines the real value of any situation, object, or person.

One evening I attended a banquet with Dr. and Mrs. Peale, who were hosting a group of corporate presidents and CEOs gathered to discuss how they might be effective in helping reestablish moral values in our society. I was seated next to the speaker for the evening, Kay Coles James. Mrs. James served as secretary of health and human services for Virginia and then, during the Bush administration, as associate director for the Office of National Drug Policy. She's a dynamic person of striking personal appearance and probing mental acuity who happens to be an African-American.

During the meal she leaned over to me and said, "I know this group isn't here to debate political issues, but I'd like to tell a story that touches on the abortion issue. Will that be a problem?"

"Is your reason for telling the story to push one position or another on the issue?" I asked.

"No," she replied. "Although my position will come out, my purpose is to show how looking at only external factors often produces wrong choices in life."

"I see nothing wrong with that," I said.

When she stood to speak, Kay Cole James told of being interviewed before the congressional panel charged with the approval of her appointment. At one point the congresswoman who chaired the panel leaned over and put forth what she called the "litmus question" regarding James's stand on abortion.

"Before I answer, let me ask you a question through the following situation. What would you say to a black woman who was barely twenty years old, single, with only a menial job and two children if she came to you and told you she was pregnant and the father had run off?"

"I would absolutely counsel her to have an abortion," replied the congresswoman. "There's no way she would be able to provide for that child and maintain any kind of support for herself and the two children she already had. The baby who would be born would have no chance at all of any quality of life and would be better off never having been born."

"Madam Chairwoman," James replied, "I'm very happy that you weren't there to counsel that young girl. You see, she was my mother and I was that third child—and my quality of life is just fine, thank you.

"Where your judgment of the situation failed was in looking at only the external factors. Those are never the most important. Yes, we lived in the housing projects; we were poor and started out with nothing. But my mother fought back from her failures, provided us with a home, and—most important—instilled in us a sense of values that made us believe we could overcome our circumstances and become anything we could dream of."

James went on to tell how when the discouragement of poverty threatened to crush her mother, that young woman's faith rose up and conquered discouragement. When the despair of the ghetto neighborhood threatened to overwhelm her, hope carried her through. When the darkness of hatred welled up in her soul, love was the sunshine that dispelled the darkness.

None of the terrible external circumstances faced by that single parent could hold back the inner power of her values.

It takes an oak tree five times as long as a willow to grow to the same size, but an oak can easily withstand the storm that knocks down every willow tree in the neighborhood. Why? Cut through the trunk of a willow tree and you'll find soft, spongy wood; cut through an oak and you'll find rock-hard heartwood. The willow has no heart; the oak does. It's what's inside, beneath the surface—the inner quality—that counts.

This principle is also deeply rooted in the Bible. When an ancient Jewish prophet was seeking to anoint a new king, candidates were brought to him based on their physical stature and appearance. Having rejected each in turn, in frustration he said, "The Lord does not look at the things man looks at. Man looks at the outward appearance, but the Lord looks at the heart" (1 Sam. 16:7).

The Cornerstone of Divinity

The third and final cornerstone of our pyramid is God. Your life will never be all that it can be, your dreams will never come true as fully as they might, without God in your life. There's no more powerful force for positive personal change in our society than the various incredibly effective programs based on the Twelve Steps of Alcoholics Anonymous. Central to every one of these programs is the recognition of the presence of, and the initiation of a search for, a relationship with God.

I spent the first portion of this chapter describing the difference between religion and spirituality. As we proceed to build our pyramid on our foundation, spirituality will be the plumb line that aligns each step of construction. Nothing more needs to be said on that subject right now, other than that I like the approach taken by one of the doctors on the currently popular television show *Chicago Hope*. Coming to a critical point in an emergency surgical procedure, he said, "Those of you who are in touch with the Infinite, now would be a good time to open communications."

"What's he talking about?" whispered one of the new doctors.

"Pray if you know how, stupid," whispered back one of the nurses.

Those communication lines to the Infinite are always open, and I'll suggest ways you can use them to find your spiritual path as we build on these cornerstones: Simplicity, Inner Quality, and Divinity. At each level we'll keep it simple, we'll look for ways to build from the inside out, and we'll explore our own spirituality.

A word about my role as we take this journey together. I claim no special power or intelligence; I'm an average American who graduated from high school and got some college under my belt. My role is not that of teacher to student but rather that of fellow student trying to solve a problem with you.

The famous author C. S. Lewis used this same analogy in his nonfiction work. Haven't we all struggled in a class sometime, perhaps staying after school to get help from the teacher? Somehow, despite everything that teacher tried, we couldn't see the answer. Why? Probably because the teacher knew too much and couldn't see the humble point from which we were beginning. Yet later, struggling over the same issue with a classmate, we were able to pool our efforts and finally "get it."

That's how I feel about this book. You and I are fellow seekers. I don't know every curve in the road ahead. There are no ultimate answers that I can share with you. There's only the knowledge that the problem has a solution, and together we can find it.

There's just one more point to keep in mind as we begin. Early one fine summer Saturday I set out on Candlewood Lake in Fairfield County, Connecticut, to do some fishing with one of my sons and a nephew who was visiting from California. Candlewood is a large lake, and we were in a canoe with a small motor, but I planned to stay for only a couple of hours and then get off the lake before the speed and pleasure boaters came out to enjoy the sunshine and water.

However, an unforeseen situation arose: we started to catch fish. As with most people who fish, this isn't normally a problem for me, and it was almost annoying to have the pleasant morning interrupted by frantic boys and flopping bass. Before I knew it, the sun was high in the sky and we had a large bay to cross to get back to the boat ramp and car.

As we approached the middle of the lake, a ski boat filled with teenagers came toward us. Apparently feeling playful, they roared completely around our little canoe, drawing a tight circle, and then shot off down the lake.

The waves from their wake came at us from all sides at once. "Get down low!" I yelled to the boys, grabbing the side of the canoe with my right hand and attempting to steer the little outboard with my left.

The rocking waves were too much, and I felt myself going over the side. In that frozen instant when the crisis hit, I saw several things at once. First, I noticed that my nephew had slipped his life jacket off in the sun, and I didn't know how well he could swim. Second, we were a long way from land. Third, I couldn't get my balance and was going over the side.

At that point I had two choices: I could hold on to the canoe and tip us all into the lake, or I could let go, fall over myself, but leave the boys afloat. If I wanted to save the situation, I had to let go of what I was clinging to for safety.

I guarantee that you'll have to let go of some past thoughts, habits, attitudes, and activities if you want to have the power behind positive thinking, as you'll discover in reading this book. So do it; let go. As in my case, you may get wet, providing a great story for someone to tell on you when those you love gather to share the tales that are the threads that hold together the fabric of a wonderful life.

Key Discoveries

Preparation

Go back to the beginning of this chapter and reread the section that defines the difference between religion and spirituality. To get the most out of this book, you must suspend your religious belief or nonbelief and focus on your personal spiritual potential. Open your mind to the possibilities, and when you return to your religion (or nonreligion), you'll have a deeper understanding of its place in your life.

Action

Take a sheet of paper and put these headings across the top: "Simplicity," "Inner Quality," and "Divinity." Then do the following:

1. List three areas of your life in which you'd like to develop Simplicity.
2. List three Inner Qualities you'd like to possess—qualities such as integrity, moral value, peace, and so on.
3. List three ways you can get to know God better—for example, prayer, meditation, the reading of scripture, or participation in a discussion group.

Now plan to reread and act on what you've written every day for a week. Perhaps the first day you'll focus on the desire to make your work more simple. Jot down any idea that comes to mind and try it out that day. On the next day commit some time to prayer, if you've listed that in the final column. Keeping at this task for a week will give you the start of a positive habit, and positive habits are the first step to personal change.

Chapter 2

Three Foundations of Spiritual Potential

Remind yourself that God is with you and nothing can defeat you. Believe that you now receive power from Him.

Norman Vincent Peale

As we begin an exploration of spiritual potential, keep in mind the themes of Simplicity, Inner Quality, and Divinity.

The simple aspect of spiritual searching is found when you realize that you don't have to look very far. Within all of us are the basics of spiritual potential. Surrounding us is bountiful evidence of divine power and grace. Ancient King David wrote, "The heavens declare the glory; the skies proclaim the work of his hands" (Psalm 19:1).

Can you watch a baby bird chip its way out of an egg and not be filled with wonder? Can you look up at the night sky, filled with billions of stars, and not marvel at the complexity of the universe? These evidences of a power beyond us are simple, yet profoundly moving.

The inner quality of our spiritual self is seen most often through emotions and feelings. From earliest childhood we have a sense of right and wrong, a sense that tells us when things are fair and when they're not, and a longing to see right and equity prevail. This longing to put the world around us into a right balance springs not from without but from within. It's a sense that drives us to sacrifice personal comfort and gain in particular circumstances. When selfish tendencies are overpowered in that way, the natural evolutionary drive to conquer is suppressed—a suppression that can't be explained physically, only spiritually.

The basic longing for a relationship with a Divine Presence is also found within and around us. Could you hear yourself involuntarily plead, "Please, dear God, let them find the survivors," after hearing of the Oklahoma City bombing, and not believe that your instinct to cry to God came from a very real place? That's the spiritual cornerstone of Divinity crying out for expression in your life.

Let's go back to our pyramid for a moment and try to visualize the model we're seeking to build. In that three-dimensional model, each of the cornerstone principles extends to form two of the three lines that make up the base of the pyramid. The figure below depicts them as seen from above.

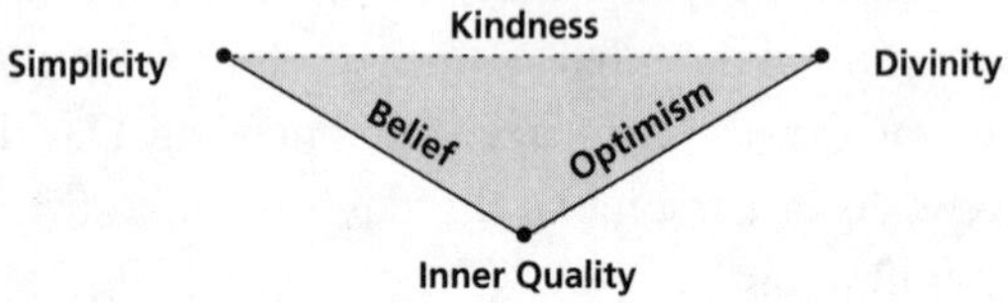

As noted in the previous chapter, the points of this horizontal triangle represent the cornerstones on which the foundations of Belief, Optimism, and Hope—the focus of this chapter—are anchored. Given opportunity and nourishment, these foundations can be built into the Faith, Hope, and Love that make a complete person.

The patterns for the foundation of deeper spirituality are planted in each of us at birth. Recognizing that God has done this planting and exploring the ways to find and follow those patterns is the focus of this book. The power to be found when we realize that God has given us this foundation is incredible.

It's a power available to anyone, regardless of race, color, creed, or national origin.

A few years ago a program called America's Awards was founded to seek out, honor, and tell the stories of thousands of ordinary citizens who were exercising their ability to overcome great odds in order to help other people. As one of the directors of this program, involved in the annual selection of recipients, I considered it a privilege to meet many of these people and to learn their wonderful stories.

When Herman Wrice grew up in West Philadelphia in the 1950s, gangs were the way to survive. He joined the Flames as a teenager and was headed into a criminal lifestyle until a priest challenged him to lead his gang from fighting into sports.

But violence was never far away, even after Herman had disavowed it. One night some gang members beat a foreign exchange student to death outside the parish gym where Herman's team practiced. That night Herman decided to devote his life to helping kids find a better way.

Soon after graduating from high school, Herman married and took a job as a cook. In his spare time he organized activities for children and founded a Cub Scout troop that soon swelled to a hundred boys.

Herman and his wife, Jean, eventually had six children of their own and "adopted" eleven more—teenagers in trouble who were placed by the courts into the family's care. Herman wanted to provide the kids with a family that loved them. Other boys stayed in the Wrice home on a less formal basis. By one count, forty Philadelphia men now call Herman "Dad."

In 1964 Herman worked with some gang leaders to form the "young Great Society." Over the next twenty years, their number grew to six hundred. These young people formed singing groups, basketball teams, and Scout troops; they rehabilitated scores of houses and established a mobile medical service and a halfway house for prisoners.

Things gradually improved until the summer of 1988, when drug dealers hooked the neighborhood's best young people. "Someone has to stop this," Herman decided, "and it might as well start with me." He talked to neighborhood men and local police and built a little "army" to chase away the dealers.

"You're crazy," the neighbors told him as the men advanced toward a group of dealers. Herman carried a sledgehammer; others carried placards that said, "We're Gonna Take Our Neighborhood Back." At the moment of confrontation, the dealers hurled threats—and ran away.

A few days later, the group stood outside the house that served as the dealers' headquarters, Herman carrying his sledgehammer. They were intent on evicting the dealers. As the neighborhood stood around to watch, the dopers leaned out the windows and taunted, "You ain't gonna to do nothin' with that hammer."

Herman wondered, "What am I doing here?" But unwilling to turn back, he lifted the hammer, ready to strike the locked front door. Just then, it was flung open and Herman walked in. At six feet four inches and 260 pounds, he looked imposing. When he and his friends moved inside, the dopers ran out the back.

For Herman, this declaration of war began a new campaign in his life. Philadelphia's mayor sent him a white hard hat with this message: "If you're going to close crack houses, you'd better wear this." Herman has worn it ever since.

Soon word reached him: "The dealers say they're gonna get you, Herman."

"Tell them I'll be at the corner of Thirty-fifth and Wallace at nine tomorrow morning," he said.

And he was. He spent all day at the corner, a neglected little park. He cut the grass, pulled weeds, and picked up litter. When he went home, he left a note giving his address and phone number, just in case they'd missed him. He wanted them to know he wasn't afraid.

The dealers didn't come, but over the next three months his car was stolen three times. During Christmas week his house was ransacked and robbed. Someone even stole his dog. Herman wouldn't retreat, however; he believed that if he stood up, others would follow.

A year later a new antidrug group seemed to be forming every week. Occasionally gunfire or an out-of-control car was aimed at the marchers, but (amazingly) no one was hurt and the numbers grew. In Philadelphia alone, more than sixty groups now wear antidrug hard hats. The movement has spread across the nation, with thousands of occasional participants and a core of hundreds of citizens who take to the streets weekly, even nightly.

And in Philadelphia, a city sometimes split by racial tensions, the antidrug coalition finds blacks, whites, Hispanics, and Asians standing vigil side by side. Dozens of drug houses have been emptied and boarded shut. Thousands of residents have gained greater peace and security. People are sitting on their front steps again.

Harvard University is examining Herman's methods as a possible model for even wider use elsewhere, and Herman has traveled to several states to talk about the program. In July 1990 President Bush praised Herman for his efforts, calling him the John Wayne of Philadelphia.

Herman Wrice knows that inner power is available to anyone in any circumstance. He won't listen when someone tells him something can't be done. Of *course* it can, if only people are willing to work. He is bigger than life—a visionary able to inspire the dispirited. The message of Herman Wrice is about looking inside yourself and finding that the incredible is possible.

The same power that Herman found can transform every area of your life, including personal, family, and business relationships. To unleash it, you need to build on the foundations of Belief, Optimism, and Kindness.

The Foundation of Belief

You wouldn't think a global moving and storage company would be a place to look for the application of spiritual power, but I know of one that is. Let me tell you about a friend who can show you the way.

David Graebel calls himself "just a trucker who got a few good loads." Today he's the chairman and CEO of Graebel Companies, which manages the moving and storage of everything from your next-door neighbor to Fortune 500 companies that transfer headquarters across the country.

A few years ago Graebel Movers—one of the Graebel Companies—was growing rapidly. Eventually the day came when the firm received its first-ever single contract for over a million dollars. Excitement spread through the six regions of the country as everyone pulled together to assemble the resources to move the client's corporate headquarters from the Midwest to Dallas, Texas.

Based on the contract, David bought six additional trucks and hired extra crews for packing, loading, and driving. The contract was the cornerstone of what was becoming his company's best year. Everything was set to begin on a particular Monday morning.

On the preceding Thursday David got what he recalls as "the worst phone call of my career."

The president of the company that had awarded the million-dollar contract called and said, "David, you've played really straight with us, so I'm giving you advance notice of a difficult situation. On Monday morning my company is going to have to seek Chapter 11 bankruptcy protection. We won't be able to honor our contract."

For a while David sat stunned at his desk. It seemed that his world was threatening to crash around him. On the basis of that canceled contract he had purchased capital equipment, hired people, and mobilized the entire company for a special effort. Backing down now was possible, but it would hurt his reputation and his ability to conduct business for a long time into the future.

"Finally I realized it was time to put my beliefs to the test," he recalls. "I came up with a plan to exercise some faith in my business. It was a key moment for me and for our team."

By Thursday afternoon the call had gone out to all six regional sales managers to fly to headquarters overnight for an emergency meeting on Friday morning. The news of the lost contract spread like a cancer, and the managers arrived clouded in doom and gloom.

David called the meeting for 9:00 A.M. He intentionally arrived late to get an overview of how the team was doing. "You never saw a gloomier bunch of people," he recalls. "No one would look at me when I came into the room; everyone was wondering who would lose his or her job first."

Smiling to himself, David strode to the head of the table and exclaimed, "Isn't this fantastic? What an incredible opportunity lies before us; I'm absolutely thrilled to be here and to have you here for this once-in-a-lifetime opportunity."

The people around the table were stunned. Several thought the "old man" had cracked up. Finally one of them spoke up and said, "Uh, boss, I thought we just lost the big contract. Why are you so excited?"

"I'm glad you asked that question," David said. "Don't you realize that just a few years ago we had only a few trucks operating out of Wausau, Wisconsin, and had barely two nickels to rub together at the end of the month? Not so long ago a million dollars was more than we made in an entire year.

"And here we are, having just lost a million dollars of business in one day, and we're still in business! In fact, we're doing so well that we can afford to fly all of you in to work out what to do about the problem.

"You all know of my deep faith in God. Well, I believe he's given us this business in order to be an example of integrity, creativity, hard work, and success. If we just clear our minds for a while, that divine power will enable us to think our way above this situation."

With that, the stunned team began to rumble: one idea came out, and then another, and finally a dozen ideas for replacing the million dollars of business were on the table. Many of the ideas were unworkable, but as the sales managers began to let go of the fear that had filled the room, faith brought two or three good ideas to the fore, and excitement filled the room.

Along the way, someone said, "You know, this is a hard business to market. There are no 'moving' magazines we can advertise in, and it's not a mass market where television and radio advertising do much good. Most of our best customers come as a result of recommendations from former satisfied customers.

"I've been thinking: there'd be no better way to get a great recommendation than to make the move we'd planned for Monday morning. Doing that on faith would sure generate more marketing publicity than we could ever buy."

David grabbed the conference room phone and called the client company's president. His first question was, "Would it help you get back on your feet if we went ahead with the move and got your headquarters relocated to Dallas?"

After a stunned silence his customer replied, "Absolutely, but that would be insane. I've already told you I can't honor the contract."

"Look," David replied, "we're more interested in having you for a long-term customer than we are in making this one deal. We're going to complete the move as planned. We'll submit the bill and get in line with the other creditors."

So Graebel Movers made the move, and the news spread through the business community faster than a computer virus. Within nine months, the company had generated nearly a million dollars in new business and had been paid 30 percent of the moving bill. But that wasn't all.

Two years later David received another call from the president of the Dallas company. "Dave," he said, "you'll recall that I phoned you in advance with some bad news a couple of years ago. Well, I wanted to call you in advance with some good news.

"Next Monday morning we'll announce that the company is coming out of Chapter 11. I've just shared the good news with our people, and we made a decision. Even though we're free of the legal obligation, we're going to work hard over the next year to repay you 100 percent of that moving job you did. It was the key to getting us back on our feet so quickly."

"This time," David recalls, "I called the team into headquarters just to celebrate! Faith had helped us move a real mountain, and that was just the beginning."

Belief stretched out into faith. That was the spiritual potential realized at Graebel Movers. In the third chapter of this book, we'll explore how you can take your own Beliefs and forge them into a faith that can defeat any problem, any fear you'll ever face.

The Foundation of Optimism

I'd like to move ahead with the second foundation of spiritual potential: Optimism that can become Hope. Hope is best seen rising out of despair, and despair is the everyday reality of many people who find themselves behind in the game of life, sometimes even before that game has really begun.

If anyone ever had a right to despair, it would be my friend Linda Owens of Richmond, Virginia. I first heard about Linda from a mutual friend who was as amazed as I have become at the story of her life. Escaping an abusive home by setting off on her own at age thirteen, Linda became pregnant at sixteen. When the father took off, she faced the first of many hard choices. She decided to keep her baby and to stay in school, determined to do whatever was necessary to accomplish those challenging goals. And she succeeded: with financial and child-care help from her church she squeaked by, working part-time jobs at a hospital and a public library to care for her daughter, LaTisha.

Life didn't get much easier. Today Linda is a single mom with four kids. Their home is an apartment in a public housing project, where gunfire rings out regularly as drug deals and gang wars claim life after life. But Linda has decided that the bad things in her life won't happen to her children.

"I did a very simple thing," says Linda. "I took a stand seventeen years ago that my children would never be denied the support I was denied. If they've needed help seeing, I've been their sight. If they've needed help trying to get to the moon, I've been their ladder.

"My children have been brought up on values—sacrifice, love, and devotion. I've cried with them, for them, and on them. Children are worth any sacrifice we can make. They weren't given the choice of whether to be born, or to whom. However, everything has a purpose. I can't determine their decisions, but I can share my values and give 100 percent of my love."

Where could she possibly have gotten that optimism? If you were to walk down Linda's street with the eyes of a cynic, you would see urban blight and decay. Rubbish gathers in the gutters. Tough-looking characters stand in the shadow of streetlights, dispensing the powders and pills that promise dreams but in the end deliver death.

In Linda's home, however, the atmosphere is completely the opposite. Bright smiles replace vacant stares. Books, magazines, newspapers, and homework are spread everywhere, and the television is generally turned off. Her four children are usually there, along with several more from the neighborhood, unless it's during the school day. The conversation is animated, the topics are stimulating, and the language is clean.

Does Linda's commitment to creating such an atmosphere work? Judge for yourself.

In 1990 her oldest daughter, LaTisha, enrolled at William and Mary College as a freshman. She was there on an academic scholarship and not only maintained the grades necessary to stay on scholarship but found her way onto two honor societies. In May 1994 LaTisha graduated summa cum laude. She was accepted at Texas A&M University's law school on a full scholarship and continues her studies today. And LaTisha's brother and sisters aren't far behind in their own pursuit of dreams that lead up and out of their humble beginnings.

Linda Owens's story perfectly illustrates how the decision to face difficulty with optimism can nurture an overpowering and ever-conquering hope. Linda's situation is an example of the crushing problems that sometime threaten to stifle us. The unemployment, poverty, hopelessness, despair, and crime that permeate her neighborhood (and many others) seem to be growing, not shrinking. Yet amid these challenges Linda and her family have simply chosen not to define their future by their past. They take stock of the problems, then face and defeat them, one at a time.

What's Linda's source of optimism and hope? If you ask her, she'll tell you that the wellhead was the spiritual strength she found in the church that helped her care for her baby and get her high school diploma so long ago. We'll explore in Chapter 4 what you can do to grow hope in your life.

Earlier in this chapter I said that the foundational elements of Belief, Optimism, and Kindness provide the basis for Faith, Hope, and Love. These elements also have an astonishing ability to cause us to suppress natural selfish tendencies in a way that can't be explained physically. This truth is nowhere more evident than in the interrelationship of the foundation of Kindness with the framework of Love—a framework built on Kindness. Before discussing this third foundational element of spiritual potential, let's explore another important, related concept.

American society in the 1990s has bought into a philosophy that fails to recognize a most important reality. We've translated the scientific understanding of nature into a false understanding of human beings. Modern scientific theory describes change as a "natural" process, shaped by genetics, environment, and time. Many people extrapolate from this view a flawed idea that human behavior is determined by similar factors. Because our personal characteristics are seen as having come our way "naturally," say supporters of this philosophy, they are to be affirmed and incorporated into what's acceptable to society as a whole.

This goes wrong, in my view, when a particular characteristic is harmful to others. Pathological behaviors, although "natural" by this definition (and therefore acceptable to those who espouse this naturalistic philosophy), should never be given legitimacy. Yet taken to the extreme, this naturalistic philosophy sees alcoholism, for example, not as a disease but as the result of genetic makeup and therefore as something inevitable and untreatable.

The truth is that humans, unlike the animal kingdom, have the ability to individually *choose* to alter their behavior. If I want to domesticate a wolf, I can; I can raise one from a cub and teach it tricks, and I'll pretty much end up with a dog. However, never in recorded history have we seen a wolf cub come in from the wild of its own volition, having decided to domesticate itself, to learn acceptable behaviors that enable it to live with humans.

This may seem a philosophical digression, but it's for a fundamental purpose. Simply put, if you buy into the modern notion that "there's nothing I can do about myself, because who I am is the result of the way [or where or when or to whom] I was born," then you might as well toss this book away. This book can't change you. Only *you* can decide to change yourself. All this book can do is provide a map and some traveling tips; you must decide to take the journey. No one can force you to take it, and no one else can take it for you. There's no such thing as "virtual reality" in this context; there are only reality and fantasy.

The Foundation of Kindness

This detour before discussing the foundational element of Kindness and its development into Love is for a special reason. I believe one of the greatest inhibitors to personal growth, spiritual understanding, and change is our distorted view of love. You see, love is not natural, and it can't be explained through naturalistic philosophy. In fact, naturalistic philosophy ultimately must exclude love as an option for human interaction.

Naturalistic philosophy is about one simple concept: the survival of the fittest by the selection of the strongest traits and the screening out of the weakest traits. This philosophy leaves no room for the concept of sacrifice for weaker or helpless beings by stronger beings.

Simply illustrated, there's no room in a purely naturalistic philosophy for my giving up the Jeep Cherokee I'd like to have to help send my three boys to college. Let them find their own way, this philosophy would urge; kick them out of the nest as soon as they can walk. If they can't thrive, then it's better that their "weak" genes be eliminated from the gene pool.

Horrible, you say? I agree. That's why a purely "do what's natural" approach is flawed. To love is *not* "natural," and yet every human society around the globe honors some expression of love as its highest ideal. We may applaud winners, but we *revere* those whose lives are defined by deeply expressed love, whether it be Shakespeare's Romeo and Juliet or India's Mother Teresa.

Put another way, survival of the fittest requires me to be, at all times, selfish and self-centered. Love, on the other hand, is the exact opposite of self-centeredness; love is *other*-centered. Dr. Peale had a great definition in his booklet *Seven Values to Live By*: "Love is the deepest desire for the good of another, regardless of the consequences for yourself."

Nice theory, but not practical in today's world, you say? Perhaps not practical, but certainly very possible.

A group of people I know founded a company called Feature Films in order to produce values-oriented entertainment that plants the seeds we're talking about. They came up with a story line about a group of kids—they call themselves the Buttercream Gang—who seek to do kind deeds for others.

You haven't seen this film in theaters, at least not yet. But it's out on video, and it's being noticed. A school group in Greensboro, North Carolina, watched it and decided to form their own real-life Buttercream Gang. They were only six kids, ages seven to nine, but one of their friends, Jennifer, was in trouble. She had recently had what was expected to be a routine tonsillectomy, but complications had set in. Although she was now doing well, the six extra days in the hospital had cost more than her family, having no health insurance, could pay.

So this "gang" of kids—Kevin, Jason, Bethany, Justin, Melanie, and Heather—came up with the idea of a yard sale to raise money for their sick friend. They sold brownies, cookies, lemonade, clothing, and other items. Their caring sparked a giving spirit that spread across the community. Consider these examples:

First a white sports car pulled up beside the yard sale, and a man got out for a glass of lemonade. As he handed Jason a twenty-dollar bill in payment, he asked why the kids were having the sale. Hearing about Jennifer, he folded his wallet and headed for his car. "Keep the change," he called over his shoulder.

Another woman paid fifty dollars for a few baked goods and two old dresses.

Then the surgeon heard of the drive and cut his bill in half, saying he hadn't been aware that Jennifer's family had no insurance.

If you or I had heard about Jennifer, we likely would have launched into a tirade, taking one side or the other in the great health care debate, demanding legislation, or laying blame on the economy, the government, or insurance companies—on anybody but ourselves. The difference between us and the Buttercream Gang in Greensboro is one thing: planting the seed of kindness and harvesting a bounty of love. That difference resulted in paid medical bills, while the typical hubbub would likely have produced nothing.

We'll explore in Chapter 5 how to develop the kindness in your own life into a deep and abiding love. The three foundational elements discussed in this chapter, along with the structures they support—Belief (supporting Faith), Optimism (supporting Hope), and Kindness (supporting Love)—create the framework of a life pyramid that's balanced, strong, and able to give strength to those around it.

Key Discoveries

Preparation

In this chapter, we've used the cornerstone principles of Simplicity, Inner Quality, and Divinity to look inside our lives and find the foundations of spiritual potential, which are Belief, Optimism, and Kindness. In seeking to understand how spiritual potential develops, we've discussed the fact that spiritual aspects of life can't be explained through a strictly naturalistic view of human development. On the contrary, we have both the opportunity and the responsibility to decide to build upon the foundational elements within us.

Action

Take a piece of paper and list three columns across the top, labeling them "Belief," "Optimism," and "Kindness." Divide each column in half vertically. On the left side of each dividing line, list the "ideal" characteristics you associate with the word at the top. On the right side of each line, list those of your own personality traits that exhibit each foundational element.

Spend some time each day for a week thinking about how you might decide to change certain attitudes or behaviors—changes that could enable you to place more of the ideal qualities into the column that defines you.

Chapter 3

Building Belief into Faith

One day in 1986 Dr. Peale asked me to come up to his office. He was working with his publisher to bring out a thirty-fifth-anniversary edition of his famous book *The Power of Positive Thinking*. We discussed the cover and other items, and then he asked, "Did I ever tell you the story of how this book got its title?"

"No, I don't think so," I replied.

"Well, my original title was *The Power of Faith*, but the editor at the time, Myron Boardman, said to me, 'Norman, do you want this book to go out only to church people or to people outside the church too?'

"I wanted it to go outside the church, of course, so Myron pointed out to me that I had repeatedly used the phrase 'positive thinking' in the manuscript, and he suggested that as the title.

"To me, then, positive thinking has always been synonymous with faith. It's faith power that works wonders."

With those few words Dr. Peale focused the introspective thinking of the previous two generations. Through the years I came to sum up his philosophy of living in the concepts of belief in yourself, belief in your family, belief in your country, and belief in your God. Dr. Peale knew that believing wasn't enough, however; action had to follow in order to produce results. The basis for action is the level of trust you have in any particular belief.

All of us are born with a basic belief in life and in the people around us. Babies know no boundaries and will often try things that can result in harm because they so instinctively believe in the world around them and seek to explore it. As we grow older, burned fingers and skinned knees teach us to temper our belief with investigation and then to trust the results. But all too often the pain of mistakes, of misplaced belief not based on investigated trust, causes the belief mechanism in people to shut down. When this happens, our growth potential is stunted, and life can take a negative path that prevents us from reaching the potential that we once imagined (and that could still be realized, were we to make our way to the right path).

Jesus knew this truth and often challenged people to begin facing their problems through the power of belief. He told those seeking a better life that they must "become like little children" (Matt. 18:3), echoing the thoughts of Isaiah, who said, "Even a little child shall lead them" (Isa. 11:6). When a distressed father came to him worried over a sick son, Jesus told him that healing would be empowered through belief. The anguished father, knowing that his fears were threatening to overpower his belief, responded, "Lord, I believe; help my unbelief" (Mark 9:24).

How can we tap into this power of belief and cause its seed to grow into faith? We must begin with our foundations. Focus first on the Simplicity of Belief. Next develop Belief as an Inner Quality. Then seek spiritual understanding of the Divinity of Belief.

The Simplicity of Belief

Belief is very powerful and yet very simple. Like the Mississippi River, which begins in my home state of Minnesota as a stream you can jump across, the longer a belief is held and the further it runs, the more strength it draws from other, related streams until it becomes a mighty, irresistible force. But even in small doses, it's powerful.

When we first moved to Pawling, New York, we found a rural community with many homes on lots of an acre or more. After a fifty-foot lot in suburban Chicago, our two acres with dozens of trees seemed like a forest preserve to me.

The previous owner of the home we bought had installed a swimming pool in the big back yard, and my three sons were fascinated by this potential. However, we moved in during March, and summer was not an immediate prospect.

Having never before investigated the intricacies of a swimming pool, in late April I began to poke around, trying to figure out its mechanisms. Without too much trouble I discovered that the pool was round, measured twenty-four feet in diameter, and was shaped by a plastic liner set into the slope of the yard on one side and exposed on the other side. There were pipes, a pump, valves, filters, and so on.

With a modest belief in my ability to deal with such contraptions, and armed with advice from a few helpful neighbors, I set about putting the pool into working order. One Saturday found me, toolbox at the ready, up to my elbows in old leaves and mucky water. I almost quit when I discovered not one but two hapless squirrels who had somehow gone for a winter swim and hadn't survived the experience—a discovery I should have been prepared for by the stench that rose up when I removed the cover.

Then came the fateful moment when I turned on the pump, believing everything to be correctly connected, cleaned out, and primed. Water sprayed everywhere, and the pump groaned like a wounded elephant. Soaked to the skin, with a muddy pipe wrench in my hand, I crawled out from behind the pool and headed across the yard to the back door. Along the way, I hurled the pipe wrench to the ground in disgust and exclaimed, "That's it; I quit."

The words were hardly off my lips when a cry of distress—the sort that can be produced only by a four-year-old in mortal fear—filled the neighborhood. I looked up to see my youngest standing on the back deck in his swimming trunks, goggles, and snorkel, carrying a beach ball. (Remember, this was still April!)

"Jon, what's wrong?" I cried, rushing to him.

"Oh, Daddy," he wailed, "if you can't fix it, nobody can!"

Remember the Popeye cartoons of the late fifties and sixties? Whenever Popeye got into deep trouble, a can of spinach would appear, and one gulp of spinach would give him superhuman power to handle the crisis. My son's absolute belief that I was the only person in the universe who could fix his swimming pool—a belief apparent in his words, his voice, and his demeanor—was like that spinach. Within the space of a few seconds I was transformed from a defeated, muddy editor who knew he had no business even owning a pool into a plumbing genius who knew nothing could stop him from living up to the belief in those eyes.

It took several phone calls for advice and at least a dozen trips to the hardware store, but one week later sparkling water gurgled softly through a functioning filtration system. And even though the water temperature was only fifty-seven degrees, the air temperature was seventy-eight, and one very happy (though almost blue) four-year-old splashed contentedly in the pool.

Silly, you say? Perhaps, but think about it. The story is absolutely true; you can ask Jon, who's now a teenager and no longer believes in my utter infallibility. He remembers that first summer, however, and we both know that the only difference between swimming and not swimming was the simple power of belief. His belief in me empowered my belief in myself, and the power of belief sustained me through the seemingly impossible.

Belief is natural when we're young. It must be nurtured and cared for as we grow older, however. Like any seed, it must be placed in good soil and given water and sunshine. In other words, whatever belief we have must be given an environment in which it can grow.

Belief as an Inner Quality

The simple things we've discussed to this point can help us begin to make belief a constant part of our lives. However, soon all of us find that pressures and tensions—especially the occasional fact of failure—hack away at our power of believing. The only way to sustain and build belief into a strong personal power is to develop it on the inside, where setbacks can't damage the framework.

When I began this book, one of my boyhood heroes, Mickey Mantle, was fighting to survive a liver transplant and stomach cancer. During that magical summer of 1961 when he and Roger Maris battled for the home-run crown, I read every word written about Mickey Mantle and listened to every interview with him I could. One question was asked over and over, and I learned from (and have never forgotten) the response.

Mickey, although he hit a lot of home runs, also struck out a lot. *Every* baseball player has an out/on-base ratio of at least two to one, but since Mickey scored big, he was questioned about his many strikeouts. He answered the question something like this: "Look, fellas. Every batter knows he's going to strike out so many times every week. I just go up there and do my best, and if I strike out, I know that's one down for this week and I'm just that much closer to a hit or a homer."

Because Mickey had internalized this conviction, he maintained his belief in his hitting ability no matter what happened on the outside (for example, strikeouts), and that produced home runs.

Dr. Peale's positive thinking philosophy is often criticized by people who claim that it offers a simplistic view of life and refuses to look at the negative, even though life is full of problems, setbacks, and troubles. Nothing could be further from the truth. Dr. Peale developed the philosophy precisely because of personal problems that he had and that he saw in others. His approach wasn't to moan over the problems, however, but to search for solutions—especially solutions that others had found—and to make that practical knowledge available to others.

His lifelong but informal study of human nature produced an astonishing conclusion. Not once, in all his acquaintance with presidents, business leaders, sports heroes, and everyday people leading happy lives, did he find a highly successful person who was basically negative. Oh, sure, every person has negative moments and tendencies. But Dr. Peale found that it was precisely the decision to fight against these tendencies and base life on belief rather than doubt that was the first step toward success.

Working for Dr. Peale allowed me to meet many of the people he saw as examples of this kind of living. One, who has become my friend and mentor, is John Y. Brown, former governor of Kentucky and present chairman of the award-winning fast-food chain Kenny Rogers Roasters.

Born in Kentucky, Brown studied law and then went into business. In his early thirties he was hired by Colonel Harlan Sanders to build his new business, Kentucky Fried Chicken. Within a few years Brown and a financial partner bought out Colonel Sanders and soon perfected the newest concept in fast food: franchising. Before long, Kentucky Fried Chicken had more stores across America than even McDonald's. Before he was forty, Brown had sold KFC and was a multimillionaire holding life by the tail.

Next came governorship of Kentucky. In that role Brown applied business principles, eliminated corruption, and put Kentucky into a fiscal condition that allowed it to thrive.

Then the "golden life" John had known began to tarnish. First came one emergency heart bypass and then another. One hip gave out and needed replacement; then the other hip gave out. Professionally, too, he struggled. After leaving the governor's office, he tried several business ventures, none of which met his expectations. When he had been out of office for nine years, he ran for governor again but lost.

"Then I decided to go back to what I know best: chicken," says John. However, success didn't come immediately. The field of fast-food chicken was crowded, and several concepts John tried showed no promise. Many of us would have given up after losing three million dollars of our own money, but not John. He had developed—and now followed—this simple, homespun philosophy: "You get your learnin' from your burnin'."

"I never spent ten minutes worrying about my heart or hip surgeries or letting a "drop foot" or a broken leg or a failed recipe slow me down. Basically, all of us have just two choices when we get up in the morning," John says. "You can either choose to focus on all the negatives and what did and could go wrong and watch that come true, or you can focus on all the positives and possibilities and work to make them come true."

Transforming Your Belief into Faith

Simple belief, developed from the inside out, is a strong starting point in developing a complete life. However, it's *only* a starting point. Only when the spiritual aspects of belief are explored does this foundation support a powerful aspect of a new and stronger personality.

Belief is the starting point for faith. All aspects of belief are contained in faith, but faith is more than belief. Jesus pointed this out to a group of intellectuals once when he said, "You believe there is one God. Good! Even the demons believe that—and shudder." (James 2:19). His point was that you can believe in something and not have faith in it. Faith leads to action, commitment, and responsibility, while belief can stop at intellectual consent.

The key element that transforms belief into faith is trust. In fact, Dr. Peale defined faith as "belief and trust in God." How does this work? There's an element of belief that goes beyond what we can see into what we simply have to trust is true.

A great example of this principle appeared in the recent film *Apollo 13*. When the outbound spacecraft malfunctioned, the crew retreated into the landing module as an emergency "life raft." As the air in that module—a craft never intended for long-term use—became increasingly unbreathable, the astronauts discovered that the filter mechanisms in the command module and the lunar module weren't compatible; one was a cylinder and the other a cube. The spares in the command module were therefore useless, and there were no spares for the lunar module (because it was to have been left behind on the moon). The technical people on the ground had only a few hours to improvise a way to filter the air so that the crew could survive days instead of hours in the tiny lunar craft.

This part of the story then focuses on those technical people—a group of dedicated scientists used to having years to consider a problem and test various potential solutions. Now they have only a few hours and are confined to the limited resources that can be scavenged from inside a crippled spacecraft thousands of miles out into space.

Rushing into a conference room carrying duplicates of materials available to the stranded astronauts, they charge at the task. They finally construct an object that will fit into the cylinder; it's made of gray duct tape, socks, a plastic bag, and filter material broken out of a spare. They *think* it will work, but it looks like something a first-grader put together with scissors and glue.

Running into the control center followed by a huddle of colleagues, the team leader carries the odd-looking object. Approaching the project director, he exclaims, "We've got it; we've got it!"

The director takes a long look, and the camera closes in on the disbelief growing on his face. He turns to the civilian technical adviser from Grumman, the company responsible for spacecraft design. "What do you think?" he asks.

Turning up his nose as if a foul smell had filled the air, the polished expert replies, "You've got to be kidding."

Looking back at the group, the director says, "Is this going to work or not? We're running out of time, and those men up there are running out of breathable air."

Silently the huddled scientists stare at one another, their feet, and the ceiling. No one wants to put his career on the line for such an improbable contraption. Finally one of the younger members—the one who had suggested the socks—says, "Sir, we don't know if it will work or not. We believe it will, and right now, that's all those men up there have. Sometimes you have to have faith."

All the power of the United States government and her biggest corporations came down to trusting in what a small group believed but couldn't prove. The belief of that huddle had to be trusted and then communicated across the miles; that trust had to be passed on to the astronauts. Only then could they follow the steps to duplicate the contraption created in the conference room. Only by faith could their lives be saved.

Earlier in this book I said that there are no magic pills or potions you can take to discover and use your spiritual potential. That's my point here too. Many times in life you have to venture into matters where there are no guarantees. A trite, superficial statement, you say? Perhaps, but nonetheless true.

Remember, I believe that life is basically quite simple. The fact that a principle such as "No guarantees" seems simplistic doesn't negate its truth. The problem with simple truths is that we tend to ignore them, not using or facing up to them when trying to live our lives.

There's just no way around it: life holds few guarantees. Therefore, there are times when your only options are to freeze or to go forward with faith. If you've built your childlike characteristic of belief into a tough adult faith, you'll be successful when you reach those times. If not, you stand a great chance of failure.

Through the years, I've had many conversations with people of faith in an attempt to discover how they built a strong faith and became successful. In every case there's been one element that stands above all others. To me, it's become the "doorway" through which everyone must pass in order to begin the process of growing simple belief into dynamic faith.

The doorway is the entrance into the darkest moments of our lives. The threshold we step over is trust, but the place into which we go is not pleasant but fearful.

Let me illustrate. While writing this chapter, I received a phone call telling me that a friend had died. Just fifty-two years old, with two kids in college, he had been told by his cardiologist just days earlier that he needed heart bypass surgery. A date was set for the following week, and he went home for the weekend to prepare.

On Saturday my friend Dave went for a leisurely walk with his wife. A quarter-mile from his home he turned red, then blue, fell to the ground, and died of massive heart failure.

Like many of their friends, we rushed over to their house to be with his wife, Lee, in those hours and days of shock after such a trauma. At one point she said to me, "Eric, I'm so mad at God for letting Dave die, and yet I know I couldn't get through the next days and weeks without my faith."

The threshold we all cross in taking intellectual belief and building it into spiritual faith is the threshold of trusting God when life sends us through a dark doorway. At those moments we want most to scream at God and ask, "What are you doing? Aren't you paying attention?" And yet it's in those moments when faith becomes the strongest and develops the most fully.

In October 1995 *Guideposts* magazine carried the story of professional golfer Paul Azinger, nicknamed "Zinger." According to that article, Zinger had once had, in his words, "the dubious distinction of being known as the best player in the world never to win a major tournament."

The year was 1993, and Zinger found himself in close contention with Greg Norman for first place in the PGA Championship at the Inverness Club outside Toledo, Ohio. He was having trouble, however, with a nagging pain in his shoulder. Two years earlier he had had an operation on that shoulder to correct a soreness. Now it was back.

Zinger played through the pain and closed to tie Norman in regular play. On the second hole of sudden death, Norman missed a difficult putt and Zinger made his to win the tournament. He was the new PGA champ! After leaping into the air, he stopped to give thanks to the Lord, recognizing God's help in his great victory.

The surging celebration of success was marred by the sharp pain he felt when he tried to lift the trophy overhead for the news cameras.

A phone call with his doctor led to a demand that he come in for an immediate biopsy. Flush with success, Zinger refused and went on to Europe to play on the winning U.S. team in the 1993 Ryder Cup competition. By the time he returned home, however, all strength was gone from his arm, so he scheduled the biopsy.

During the week that they waited for the test results, Zinger and his wife reflected on their lives. At thirty-three years old, he was at the peak of his career. With Toni and his two daughters, he had the family everyone dreams of. But the specter of death now haunted him.

Going to the doctor for the results, Zinger wasted no time. "How am I?" he demanded.

Looking him right in the eye, the doctor responded just as directly: "Paul, you have cancer."

Zinger recalls the moment: "Toni gripped my hand and I rocked back and forth in my chair, shaking my head. I had been worried about my career, not about dying. Suddenly everything had changed."

Rushing to the bathroom, Zinger got sick, and in his despair he cried out, "Lord, help me! I'm scared to death."

The next few days brought appointments with cancer specialists and the scheduling of surgery. Finally Zinger and his wife and children retreated to a hotel to wait through the weekend. He began to reflect on the place of faith in what he was about to experience. First he remembered how much closer he had felt to God during the early years of his career, when things were hard.

"Sometimes it is when you have the least that you are most aware of how much the Lord provides. We always managed to put enough food in our mouths and gas in the camper and looking back that trust seemed so important."

On the Sunday morning of that difficult weekend, a local church held its services in the hotel ballroom. Zinger and his family went, and something about the service touched him: "I felt face-to-face with God, and an excitement I hadn't felt in years came over me. I knew that Christ wanted not just my cancer, or my golf, or my fears about my family, but all of it—my whole life, if only I would give it to him and recommit myself to faith. *I need you more than ever, Lord,* I whispered silently."

Throughout the process of seeing specialists, scheduling surgery, and preparing for chemotherapy, Zinger was struck by this paradox of faith becoming stronger in the darkest hours of his life. His fears were still there, however, and he often worried about what would happen if he didn't survive.

"Then one morning while I was getting ready for the day, something happened. I was standing in my bedroom praying, wondering in the back of my mind what would happen if I didn't get better. The sun was forcing its way through the blinds when suddenly a powerful feeling swelled over me like a huge, gently rolling wave, lifting my feet off the sandy bottom of the sea.

"I stopped everything I was doing and experienced an incredible peace-giving sensation. I knew that God was with me; I felt absolutely assured that I would be okay. It wasn't that God told me what would happen next, or that the cancer would go away. I simply felt positive I was in his complete and loving care no matter what."

Now, three years later, Zinger is still cancer-free and has a new purpose to life, a purpose for others: "What keeps me going these days is the chance to be an example for others who are struck by disease, to help them see that God is there for them no matter what. That's all you need to know to get through anything in life. That is the real 'major.'"

Paul Azinger stood on his foundation of Belief and built it, through trust, into a powerful Faith. If you follow his example, you'll construct the first of three supports that begin to give shape to your life pyramid. When each of these supports—first Faith, then Hope, and finally Love—is in place, you'll have the elements of a complete life.

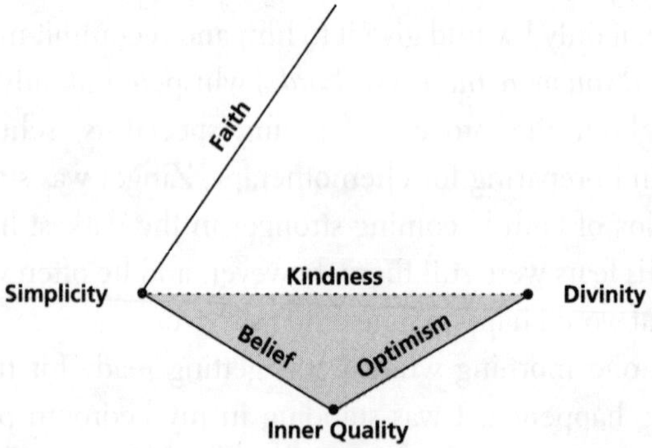

Bringing these elements into balance and strengthening each one becomes a lifelong process of growth and discovery.

Key Discoveries

Preparation

In this chapter we've explored how to go about taking our natural belief and building it into a powerful faith. In order to examine the process, we've used the cornerstones of Simplicity, Inner Quality, and Divinity to consider aspects of the building process. As will be true of every key principle in this book, your own power of choice is vitally important in the development of faith. In the end, we have tremendous power over the direction of our lives, because we choose how to respond to each and every situation. We often can't choose the situations, but we always can choose our response.

Choosing faith is sometimes difficult. Think back to the *Apollo 13* story. All of those engineers and scientists had to give up a lot of personal ego and years of training to place their belief and trust in duct tape, a plastic bag, and socks. But when you come right down to it, only by choosing faith at such moments will we be able to survive and thrive.

Action

1. *Create a mental climate of believing.*

You can reshape your thinking by choosing to fill your mind with belief thoughts. A simple technique is to start each day by saying, "I believe, I believe, I believe."

Next, memorize a simple passage from the Bible that affirms the power of believing. My favorite is "Everything is possible for him who believes" (Mark 9:23). Write it on a card, carry it in your pocket or purse, and say it over and over throughout the day.

2. *Practice believing on simple terms.*

The easiest way to grow your power of belief is to practice it. Start simply. At work, set out on Monday affirming, "I believe I can make one extra sale this week" or "I believe I can finish this report early to have more time for the next project."

For this to work, you have to throw out all the weasel words—words such as *maybe, if only, can't,* and so on. Once you've practiced on a simple matter, as in the above examples, raise the stakes and move forward.

3. *Add up your assets.*

Once a friend of Dr. Peale's who had experienced a business reversal rushed into his office exclaiming, "I'm ruined; I've lost everything!"

Dr. Peale replied, "I'm sorry to hear that your wife and children died, your house burned down, and you've been diagnosed with incurable cancer and given only two months to live."

"What are you talking about?" the man demanded. Then, after a moment of thought, he said, "Oh, I get it. I still have a lot of assets, don't I?"

Add up your assets: friends, family, health, job, good mind, ideas, commitment.

4. *Take time each day to think about God.*

A golfer spends time thinking through his or her game. A writer thinks through each sentence before putting fingers to the keyboard. In the same way, we need to stop to look up at the sky, toward the trees, or into the face of a baby in order to feel the vastness of the universe and the presence of the power that created it.

5. *Memorize a great spiritual quote.*

As a Christian, my favorite is this: "I can do all things through Christ, who strengthens me" (Phil. 4:13). Written by the apostle Paul to a church at Philippi, it helps me verbalize the trust I want to have, thereby pulling energy toward realizing that desire.

Chapter 4

Building Optimism into Hope

The natural optimism born into a baby is one of the most powerful forces on the planet. What allowed Thomas Edison to discover the filament that would allow him to create the lightbulb after hundreds of failures? How could Jim Abbott possibly pitch in the major leagues with one arm? Where did Gandhi get the power to single-handedly bring a world power to its knees with nothing more than his spirit? What force drove John Johnson out of Chicago's housing projects to found *Ebony* and *Jet* magazines and the Black Entertainment Network?

The seed of positive expectation, or optimism, was nurtured in each case until it grew into unstoppable hope. This chapter is about how you can nuture your own optimism and discover the same power. This chapter is also the place where many readers will fall away. No single concept in positive thinking is more misunderstood and misrepresented than that of optimism.

Early in the publishing history of Norman Vincent Peale's famous book *The Power of Positive Thinking*, critics often wrote descriptions like this one: "A rosy-colored false view of the world filled with 'Pollyannish' optimism." (Remember the book *Pollyanna* and its movie follow-up? The name belonged to the main character, a young girl who looked for the best in everything, even when others thought she was being ridiculous. In the end, through the magic of storytelling, her view came true.)

"Let's get real," the critics said, in effect. "Wishing doesn't make something happen. People who go blindly through life simple-mindedly expecting things to get better will fail and drag down others who are being 'realistic' and facing up to their problems."

What the critics missed, in both *Pollyanna* and Dr. Peale's book, was the fact that optimism (or the more overarching concept of positive thinking) doesn't mean that a person fails to face problems; instead, optimism offers a successful technique for *confronting* and *overcoming* problems.

America is a nation that runs on the business of business. Our incredible standard of living and unbelievable opportunities for any person to succeed are based on a capitalistic economy where market forces and the responses to them drive success or failure.

My role at the Peale Center has given me special opportunities to meet some of the most successful business leaders of our day. We seek out their advice on projects and prepare publications filled with stories drawn from their practical experience.

Whether it's a leading computer company, a successful fast-food organization, a moving and storage giant, a top publisher, a Midwest manufacturer of premier cutting tools, or the men and women who run these firms, all have one trait in common: no top company or successful executive ever got to the top by being negative. True organizational leaders are infused with a natural optimism that makes them rush at seemingly insurmountable problems and go over, around, under, or straight through to success.

I challenge anyone reading this book to send me the story of a single person with a basically negative view of life who has accomplished any great achievement. *All* achievers are optimists. They see the opportunity in every crisis, the power in every problem. So if you want to build a life that overcomes instead of goes down in defeat, look to their examples. Learn the secrets of using your natural optimism to marshal the forces around you into a successful pattern.

Perhaps Norman Vincent Peale said it best in the introduction to his best-selling book *The Tough-Minded Optimist:* "When you have what it takes to deal creatively with the harsh facts of human existence and still keep on believing in good outcomes, you are a tough-minded optimist."

An awful lot of truth is imbedded within that statement. "Having what it takes" is a condition that each of us can develop; it's not something we're born with or not. "Dealing creatively with the harsh facts" of living this life certainly doesn't sound like a formula for whistling in the dark and avoiding problems. Life can be tough; it inevitably throws all of us curves once in a while. The ability to be ready for those curves and to handle them creatively springs from optimism regarding the possibility of a good outcome.

And finally, the ability to keep that positive outlook—to "keep on believing in good outcomes"—is the key to success over problems. Optimism doesn't simply offer a rose-colored view of the world; it's a time-tested, success-proven, scientifically demonstrated method of solving problems. It's exciting to see reports of this scientific discovery appearing more and more in the popular press.

In the June 1994 issue of *Prevention* magazine, the editors reported on an article in the medical journal *Lancet* announcing that researchers had discovered that Chinese-Americans who were born in a year believed to be ill-fated for certain diseases died as many as four years earlier than either Chinese-Americans whose diseases and birth years didn't match or Anglos who had the same diseases but more optimistic beliefs.

The study leader, David P. Phillips, a professor of sociology at the University of California, San Diego, concluded the following: "This suggests that by changing your mood or expectation, you might be able to live longer, not shorter.

"Our findings and those of others suggest that mental attitude is associated with health. Changing your attitude doesn't require a physician—it's something you can do on your own. In many ways, you have a greater ability to affect your longevity than your physician does."

Other health professionals also point out the value of optimism early in life. Writing about parenting in *Chatelaine* magazine in January 1993, writer Rona Maynard referenced the studies done by American psychologist Martin Seligman showing that optimistic kids have a lifelong advantage over pessimistic children. Their strength lies not in their genes but in an attitude toward life that other kids can learn. Wendy Brennan, a Canadian psychologist, found that optimistic kids explain a problem to themselves using three mental habits that give them an edge:

1. They see the problem as temporary. They figure that new or practiced effort will overcome the difficulty.
2. They don't take problems or setbacks personally. They don't call themselves stupid for failures or mistakes.
3. They don't let setbacks poison their lives. An optimist passed over for a part in the school play, for example, will volunteer to work on costumes or props.

Let's put this problem-solving perspective to work on the concept of optimism as we view it through the cornerstone principles of Simplicity, Inner Quality, and Divinity.

The Simplicity of Optimism

Optimism provides a simple way for anyone to get started on the most difficult problem in his or her life. An example I'll never forget is Marsha Altheizer of Dallas, Texas.

A group of us from the Peale Center went to Dallas to film some people who had written to us about how the power of positive thinking had changed their lives. One letter had come from Marsha, a vivacious thirty-something woman who ran one of the largest portrait photography studios in the Dallas metro area. I couldn't imagine what her story would be, since she seemed to have it all: a dynamic personality, a successful business, and a beautiful and intelligent twelve-year-old daughter.

"Oh, I wasn't always this successful," Marsha told me. "Eleven years ago I was a young mother who hadn't finished high school, who had an infant daughter, and whose husband had just walked out on us, leaving us no money and no place to live.

"For weeks I survived on welfare and borrowed money. I borrowed money for gas for the car, for formula for my baby. I was terribly down and so depressed. Then someone gave me some audiotapes on positive thinking.

"From the tapes I got the idea that if I would just clear my mind of all the negative thoughts, angers, and disappointments, then my mind could be receptive to ideas to help me out of my problems.

"Well, this was entirely new to me at the time. The concept of believing in a good outcome was a brand new way of thinking.

"Since I had no money and no job, I helped out friends who helped me by driving their kids places or taking them shopping. After a while I found myself taking several kids to daycare every day. I'd be listening to those tapes as I drove and trying to clear my mind for some idea of how I could get me and my daughter out of the spot we were in.

"One day, as I was waiting at the daycare center, another mother came up to me and showed me the school picture taken of her first-grader. It was a nice, standard school picture, nothing special—but then she made a comment that changed my life: 'You know, Marsha,' she said, 'I wish they took pictures like these here at the daycare center. It would be nice to have the same type of picture of my younger child to send to the grandparents.'

"Because my mind was open," said Marsha, "I thought to myself, 'I wonder why they don't do that,' and then, 'I bet *I* could learn how to do that!'"

With that creative spark, born of learned optimism, this single, undereducated, and jobless mother began to ask questions. She found out that all the public schools contracted with one or two big photographic companies to do their school photos, so that market was closed to her. However, those same big companies apparently thought that the twenty to thirty nearby daycare facilities were too small to be profitable for them; they didn't bother to market their product to those facilities.

"I didn't even know how to load a camera," Marsha recalls, "but I knew I loved children and could get them to smile for a picture, and I knew that mothers would be thrilled to buy such a picture. I also had found a formula through listening to the tapes on positive thinking."

"What was that formula?" I asked.

"*You* should know," Marsha said with a laugh. "It's the simple formula of faith in God, followed by faith in myself and a lot of hard work on the ideas God gives."

With a little more borrowed money, Marsha began her business. At first she was learning, and it took so much time that she didn't make much money. But she studied everything she could find on photography and found good suppliers for film and developing. She also learned that by doing the work herself rather than relying on a (nonexistent) staff, she could be competitive on price. Best of all, since she was in daycare centers all day, her daughter could come to "work" with her.

Soon the business grew. In the course of her daycare work, Marsha learned that many families had other pictures they would like taken, so she set up a portrait studio for adult photos, pet photos, sibling photos—the list became endless.

"At first I would sit down every day and imagine my appointment book so full that I just couldn't take another shoot," Marsha recalls. "Then it began to *happen*, and I expanded until we now shoot hundreds of daycares a year in the Dallas–Fort Worth area and are certainly the biggest photographic studio of this type."

Today Marsha's studio employs several people, a couple of them struggling single mothers. Her business has provided for her and her daughter. More important, it's given her a faith in herself that can't be taken away by problems not seen today.

By the way, do you want to know the name of her studio? Would you believe "Positive Images"?

The simple "atmosphere of optimism" that Marsha created by choosing to believe in the possibility of a good outcome enabled her to see an opportunity others had missed. If she had decided to live in fear and regret, or in anger and blame toward her former husband, the success she knows today would never have been hers. Without resources, education, or even knowledge of photography, Marsha energized the world around her through her optimism, and a marvelous result was created.

Marsha's story is a prime example of one of the central principles of positive thinking: the law of supply. Based on the reality that faith and effort create an atmosphere in which success can grow, the law of supply states three important premises:

1. Commit yourself to work with a talent God has given you or on a project God needs done.
2. Do your best with what you have, and more will flow to you.
3. Put the project in God's hands and work as hard as you can.

When you follow these three steps, the law of supply is activated. As a result, all you need in order to keep moving forward comes to you at the time you need it. The more faithful you are—faithful in the ways that Marsha was—the more the supply increases and overflows.

There's a story recorded in the Bible—one told by Jesus—that affirms this powerful principle. Found in Matthew 13:3–9, it goes like this: "A farmer went out to sow his seed. . . . Some seed fell on good soil, where it produced a crop—a hundred, sixty, or thirty times what was sown." Jesus noted that seed dropped on hard or rocky ground or in a weedy area failed to produce, but the seed planted on good ground gave, at a minimum, a thirty-fold yield. That's 3,000 percent! And remember, that's the *minimum*; some seeds produced 10,000 percent.

The trick is to plant your seed of optimism in good soil. How? Simply by following the steps Marsha took in her photography business. First, commit yourself to work with a talent God has given you or on a project God needs done. A good technique for finding yourself committed to your own talent is to make an estimate of your abilities and then raise it 10 percent. This realizable goal energizes you to get to work.

Second, do your best with what you have, and more will flow to you as you need it. Time and again I've talked to people who said they were ready to get started on a path of fulfilling their dream, only to find out they were *waiting*—waiting for the right time or for more money or for a commitment from someone else. The key is to get started *yourself*.

Finally, put the project in God's hands and work as hard as you can. Being single and having a baby to care for, Marsha might not have worked as hard as someone in more comfortable circumstances could, but she worked as hard as she could.

This book is a great example of these techniques in action. I knew I had enough writing talent to put down two hundred pages or so of thoughts on the power behind positive thinking. What I was *not* sure about was my ability to do so in a manner that would attract a publisher and a reading audience. That was the part I had to raise 10 percent.

Once I got started, I found myself cleaning my desk, waiting for a friend to comment on the first paragraph, or waiting for a publisher to comment on my book outline and first chapter. I had to accept the estimate and get on with the work.

Many times people are just afraid of good, hard work. One recent weekend Joy and I drove to Pennsylvania to spend some time with our friends John and Faye Smith. Several years ago John was working for a company that sold items such as pens and coffee mugs with the logo or advertising message of the customer printed on the item. After a few years of working for someone else, John began to get ideas about how to build a bigger business, and he struck out on his own.

For several years it was tough. "Our oldest daughter used to tell her friends that her family had money until her daddy started his own business!" John recalls. But John persevered, and Faye joined him. After a few years the business thrived and grew.

Today there are several employees, including salespersons who work on commission, which means they get paid according to what they sell. One day John was trying to figure a way to build the business without hiring more people and at the same time allow his employees a share in the success they were helping to build. Doodling with his pencil, he came up with the idea that if they all worked one hour longer each day, over their average of 220 working days per year, they'd work an extra month per year. In effect, the company would get thirteen months of sales in a calendar year! Better still, with extra commissions for extra sales, the staff would get an extra paycheck every twelve months.

Excited, John shared his idea with the sales team. Although the sales reps looked thoughtful, not much was said. One or two seemed to get the idea, but the concept of extra work didn't generate much enthusiasm. He couldn't figure it out. One hour per day, why that was nothing—skip a television show or set the clock thirty minutes earlier and stay thirty minutes longer at night. Didn't they see the potential?

Apparently not. Imagine John's shock when one of the sales team confronted him the next day. "I've been thinking about this hour-a-day thing, boss," the salesman began tentatively.

"Great!" John exclaimed.

"Well, you see," the man continued, "I've actually been thinking about reversing your idea. That is, I'll work an hour less every day, get the same amount done, and have another month a year to relax!"

Turned upside down, a good idea walked away from optimism and fell into a pessimistic approach that would get that salesman more free time but in the end would deprive him of a future of increased financial freedom. Taken to the extreme, this man's selfish view would wind up holding him back.

Optimism as an Inner Quality

We're born with a natural optimism that can be eroded over time if we don't nourish and cultivate the seed. Like belief, optimism is a quality that begins inside us and needs to be built into the full framework of Hope.

Our core attitudes shape the way we either develop or retard our natural tendency toward optimism. Those attitudes are born of repeated thoughts in a particular direction. For instance, one person in an economic situation that needs improving may be inclined to look for solutions, while another in the same situation tells himself it can't get better (even though this latter approach can't do any good). My friend John—the one with the team of sales reps—has done well in his company for many years, through good and bad times. When I asked him why, he replied, "It's simple. Any successful salesperson has to be an optimist, because if you aren't, you can't face all the rejections and keep going out until that next sale is made."

An authority no less than the *Wall Street Journal* believes that individual optimism is the driving force behind much of the United States' economy:

> *Despite an improved economy and stepped-up volunteer programs, Americans are increasingly worried about their financial future. . . . As soon as people* feel confident *that this economy is strong, it will last.*
>
> Oct. 19, 1994, page A8; italics added

A paraphrase for the conclusion of that *Wall Street Journal* article? It's what's inside that counts. The nation's greatest business journal asserts that even a numerically healthy economy can't sustain momentum unless the people driving and living with that economy gain and exercise optimism about the future.

How, then, do we build on the foundation of Optimism that lies within us? What do we do when the circumstances of our lives have robbed us of the ability to feel confident—an ability that's vital to economic and personal achievement? I suggest a simple method taught by Dr. Peale.

He used to tell about his fifth-grade teacher, who would write the word *can't* on the blackboard and then turn to the class and ask, "What's wrong with that word?" He taught them to respond by shouting, "Erase the *t*; erase the *t!*

"That's right," the teacher would reply. "If you think you can't, you won't. If you think you can, you will."

Try using the word *can* in this simple exercise for rebuilding your optimism. Take a sheet of paper and write the word like this:

C hoose

A nother

N otion

Put the paper in a place where you can see it often—on your bathroom mirror, kitchen refrigerator, or car sun visor. Each time you see it, think through the meaning.

Choose: Our power to choose is greater than any force in the universe. Every step downward or upward in life begins with a choice. Has your spouse said an angry word this morning? You choose to respond with anger or love. Is there a problem at work today? You choose to either face it or ignore it. Is there a chance to underreport income on your tax forms? You choose either honesty or dishonesty.

Another: One of the greatest lessons I've learned in life is that there are always other options. Never accept the statement, "The only thing we can do is . . ." Always stop and look for other options. When you suggest something, people are likely to say, "But we've never done it that way before." Don't automatically accept that response as a veto.

Recently my church was looking for ways to control the monthly expenses. Every idea involved cutting back some program that was serving our families or our community, and no one wanted to take those options. Finally someone said, "What about the mortgage?" The instant response was, "We *have* to pay the mortgage; there's nothing we can do there." We stuck with the idea, however, and uncovered the fact that we could cut 3 percent from the interest rate by refinancing. A meeting that started with gloomy expectations of reduced programs ended in joyful celebration. The only one who wasn't happy was our banker.

Notion: Every choice in life begins with an idea. Every great success in life begins with an idea. McDonald's was built on the notion of "consistent quality in a clean atmosphere." Ford Motor Company took its own slogan—"Ford has a better idea"—to heart and made "Quality is job one" into the driving force behind the best-selling car of the 1990s, the Taurus. Choose to think in a new way, and you unlock tremendous power in any area of your life.

Once you've rediscovered your natural optimism and begun the process of activating it in your life, you'll find that it must be built into hope to sustain you. Natural optimism will take you only so far. Sooner or later, life will hand you a tragedy you can't handle unless you've grown optimism into the divine quality of hope.

Transforming Your Optimism into Hope

This chapter began with economic examples of the power of optimism, but economic success isn't all there is. One goal of this book is to enable you to see how all of life is knit together. The spiritual elements of life aren't separable from relationship elements, intellectual elements, or business elements.

The greatest investment strategist of our generation, Sir John Marks Templeton, is a tremendous optimist on the future of the economy. In remarks in a speech titled "The Economic Future," given to shareholders of Templeton Mutual Funds in October of 1992, he said:

> *With the fall of Communism and the sharply reduced threat of nuclear war, it appears that the U.S. and some form of an economically united Europe may be about to enter the most glorious period in their history. Business is likely to boom. Wealth will increase. By the time the twenty-first century begins, I think there is at least an even chance that the Dow Jones Industrial Average may have reached six thousand, perhaps more. Despite all the current gloom about the economy and about the future, more people will have more money than ever before in history.*
>
> *The doomsayer misses the overriding fact that there is a Creator behind this drama, moving our world and us to bring an ever greater revelation of his goodness and concern for his creation.*

Read that last paragraph again. If you were seeking out an investment counselor to manage your life savings of ten thousand dollars, can you honestly say that you would choose someone who was relying on a Creator who had "goodness and concern for his creation"?

Yet if you had placed that ten thousand dollars in the Templeton mutual fund when it was founded in 1954, you would have had more than eight hundred thousand dollars today—the finest performance of any fund of its kind.

The key to Sir John's application of the optimism principle is his spirituality. He's gone beyond simple optimism by applying his knowledge of the presence and power of God in a business situation.

Hope, then, means going beyond our own optimistic efforts. Hope can be defined as "the expectation of divine support for success." By cultivating that expectation within yourself, you place yourself on the path of divine guidance.

In the Judeo-Christian tradition, this source of hope is deeply ingrained in thousands of years of teaching about God. The key spiritual distinction of this tradition is a belief in a personal God who knows and cares for individuals. That care is revealed through promises.

The Bible is filled with such promises, but none is more direct than Jeremiah 29:11: "For I know the plans I have for you," declares the Lord, "plans to prosper you and not to harm you, plans to give you hope and a future."

If faith is belief and trust in God, then hope is the exercise of that faith in the practical areas of life—in our relationships, our work, our communities, and our health. Without faith, there can be no true hope. Likewise, unless we nurture the seed of natural optimism to grow into hope, that seed will die.

How, then, do we focus the nurturing process? Another simple acrostic can be helpful:

H onest

O ptimism

P ractically

E xercised

Optimism, in order to grow into hope, must be based on both fact and faith. Marsha Altheizer's decision to open a photography studio was based on the fact that schools take pictures of children and mothers buy extra prints of those pictures. Her faith was that she could learn a new skill and exercise that skill to build a business. The exercise of that optimism must be practical; it must be something that can be undertaken. Flying a Boeing 747 isn't practical for me, but taking flying lessons is.

Finally, hope comes from optimism exercised. Faith begins more often in the mind, while hope begins in the hands. Do something hopeful, and your hope will grow. Take action for a positive result or against a negative situation, and the first steps of that action will result in power for the next steps.

One crisp September Saturday—a foggy day—I took two of my sons fishing early in the morning. We decided to let the boat drift with the breeze and fish a shoal near the landing. As was usual when the kids were young, I spent the first thirty minutes rigging their lines, positioning the boat, and sounding the horn to avoid hitting any other early fishing fanatics.

By the time I started to fish, Jon had put down his pole and was munching on doughnuts and playing in the water. Rather than taking the time to rig my own rod, I picked up his and began casting. Suddenly I had a strike. It was the biggest small-mouth bass I'd ever hooked! With much yelling and scrambling, we somehow managed to net the prize a few minutes later. When we'd calmed down, we measured it at twenty-one inches and weighed it at five pounds four ounces.

Jon exclaimed in frustration, "Dad, why do *you* catch all the fish?"

That question has bugged children for generations. How can Dad always catch the biggest fish when he seems to do more rowing, baiting, and untangling than anything else? When I was little, my dad always caught the fish, and now I was catching them with my boys. "Well, Jon," I replied, "I guess because I keep my line in the water. You can't catch fish while eating doughnuts."

I remember hearing within those words a great lesson for myself when we got back on shore. Success in any endeavor is 90 percent hanging in there. Hope grows from optimism when we exercise it, practice it, and keep at it through all the moments when the results are thin.

Our life triangle is now beginning to take shape. Starting with the base formed by the three foundations of Belief, Optimism, and Kindness, we first examined how to build on the foundation of Belief to provide the support of Faith. In this chapter the foundation of Optimism is built upward to create the support of Hope, as the diagram below illustrates.

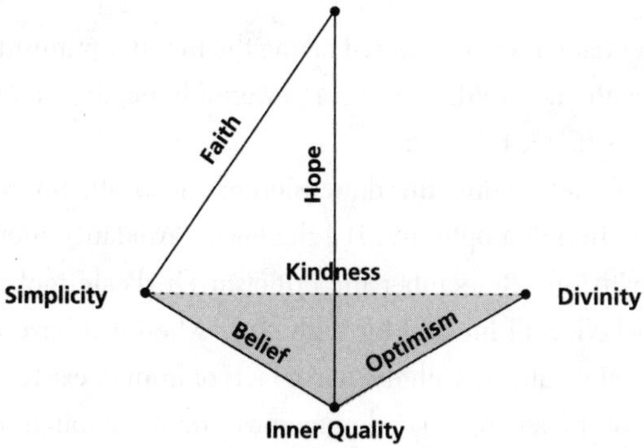

Key Discoveries

Preparation

In this chapter we've explored taking the inborn optimism we all start out with and building it into a powerful hope, the expectation of divine assistance for success.

Key to understanding this dimension of our spirituality is facing the false notion that optimism is a shallow or avoidance method of dealing with life. Remember the criticism Dr. Peale took for his Pollyannish view of life and his reply that "when you have what it takes to deal creatively with the harsh facts of human existence and still keep on believing in good outcomes, you are a tough-minded optimist."

Marsha Altheizer's formula for optimistic achievement is a great practical example of Dr. Peale's point: "Faith in God, followed by faith in myself and a lot of hard work on the ideas God gives in response to my faith."

As with faith, build your childlike optimism into a tough adult hope, and you'll strengthen every aspect of your life.

Action

1. Write out the two acrostics given in this chapter and put them in your daily appointment calendar or some other place where they can easily be seen every day:

C hoose

A nother

N otion

and

H onest

O ptimism

P ractically

E xercised

2. Faith is helped most by thinking and reading. As we "grow" hope, we must take concrete action, and one of the best actions I know is to write things down. Get a notebook of any type that appeals to you and title it "My Spiritual Journey." Use it to begin recording suggestions in this book and other ideas that come to you. Specifically to build hope, pick three characteristics about yourself that you would like to develop and write them under two columns: one headed "Realistic Estimate"; the other headed "10 Percent Goal."

In the first column, be honest about where you are; in the second, raise your estimate of your ability to improve by 10 percent and write it down. Refer back to this chart each week until the goal is achieved, and then raise it another 10 percent. You'll find what all philosophers have taught: each of us is capable of infinitely more than we imagine. The way to realize that potential is to begin in 10 percent steps.

3. Write out another strong spiritual quote to help build your hope. My favorite is the Jeremiah quote I shared earlier: "For I know the plans I have for you," declares the Lord, "plans to prosper you and not to harm you, plans to give you hope and a future."

Chapter 5

Building Kindness into Love

Kindness is the greatest, yet the most fragile, of the spiritual seeds planted within us at birth. It has the astonishing potential to grow into an enormous power, yet it often dies from neglect before it has a chance to sprout.

Kindness is also uniquely human. For example, humans are the only creatures who routinely feel compassion for, and take responsibility for raising, the young of others. Pictures of starving and mistreated children have motivated millions of people to donate time and money to relieving that suffering. Air strikes were undertaken in Bosnia and infantry troops committed to Somalia largely because of suffering children. Public outcry, motivated by natural kindness, produced a public policy result of battlefield aggression—seemingly the opposite of kindness.

Kindness that grows into love is the most deeply spiritual of the seeds within us. One can see the benefits of belief or optimism and make use of those benefits without much regard for their spiritual dimensions. One cannot go very far into the exploration of kindness and love, however, without encountering deep spirituality.

Earlier I discussed how one of the great evidences for spiritual truth is the presence of spiritual factors that can't be explained through "natural" truths. The natural concept of survival of the fittest is violated over and over by the spiritual forces of kindness and love. If this weren't so, every charity in America would go out of business tomorrow. Not another hurricane survivor would find shelter from the Red Cross, not another hungry family would find food at Second Harvest, not another heart patient would be helped through donations to United Way. It doesn't make sense *naturally* to give up food or money to help weaker people. Spiritually, though, it makes all the sense in the universe.

The power of kindness built into love can overcome the most difficult, even apparently impossible, situations.

When I speak to high school young people, I often ask them to raise their hands in response to this question: "How many of you think you have a tougher time period to grow up in than your parents had?"

Invariably nearly every hand goes up. Then I tell them the tale of 1968.

I was in high school in 1968. It's the most awful year in my memory. In January the North Vietnamese launched the Tet Offensive, and more young Americans were killed in battle in the next two weeks than at any other time in Vietnam. In February a Navy ship named *Pueblo* was captured by the North Koreans, and for months we watched television pictures of young sailors and their officers held hostage and tortured. In April Martin Luther King, Jr., was assassinated, and in June Bobby Kennedy was gunned down.

Then came the summer. In 1992—over twenty years after the year I'm describing—a portion of Los Angeles erupted in riots, burning, and looting that lasted for three days, while in 1968 seventeen cities burned not for three days but for most of the summer. Living in a Minneapolis suburb, I was able for a time to think that this trouble was far away—Chicago, Atlanta, Los Angeles. Then I got up one morning to see a front-page article—complete with disturbing picture—of a car bomb and fire on Hennepin Avenue, just twelve miles away.

In 1968, in the middle of the turbulent Watts district of Los Angeles, there lived a woman named Alice Harris. Born in Gadsden, Alabama, she had become pregnant at thirteen and dropped out of school. She drifted from there to Detroit, where she later married and had more children. In 1959 she and her husband moved to Los Angeles to find better opportunities. Today she runs a program, born out of the rioting, that has made her one of my favorite "American's Awards" winners.

During the riots of 1968 Alice ran among the looters, dragging children home so that they wouldn't be killed in the fires that burned entire city blocks. She saved many lives. Following the riots, urban planners held a meeting in Watts. After the consultants unveiled their plans, Alice rose to speak: "Gentlemen, what Watts needs most is a medical clinic. It takes an hour and a half on the bus to get downtown to the hospital. Three weeks ago, a six-year-old boy was hit by a car while crossing the street. It took three hours for the ambulance to arrive."

Right then and there the planners added an emergency health center to their proposal. Buoyed by her success, Alice began speaking out on behalf of young people. One month later she founded Parents of Watts (POW) to address the needs of her neighbors.

If people needed a place to sleep, she found shelter. If they needed food, she provided it. If they needed a brighter future for their children, she created it. Whatever someone asked, Alice responded with an attitude that said, "Oh, yes, I can!" She never said no to anyone in need. "I never want to hear no," she explains. "No is all these people have ever heard. When someone finally says yes and helps you, hope comes alive."

By the time 1991 rolled around, Alice presided over fifteen programs operating out of seven houses POW owns along Lou Dillon Avenue. Most of the programs get government food and shelter funds. The rest of her needs are supplied by small donations from many people, including regular contributions from her husband, Allen, a pipe fitter.

When the recent rioting started, Alice's program was smack in the middle of five housing projects in south-central Los Angeles, the area hardest hit. In her immediate neighborhood, however, there were no fires and minimal looting. Bernard Parks, who was Los Angeles's deputy chief of police at the time, gave Alice's work over twenty-five years as the reason more damage hadn't been done. "I wish we had a couple more thousand in our city like Sweet Alice," he said.

Alice is called *Sweet* Alice because she's just that. She looks stern from a distance, but up close there's a warm kindness about her, a sense of caring and openness that welcomes those in need. There's a firmness couched in Alice's sweet manner as well, however. "We aren't running a free motel here," she tells those who seek help. "Everybody has to do his share."

People who come to Alice's homes get a long-term commitment that includes not only food and shelter but also personal counseling, legal and drug counseling, schooling, and assistance with job placement. Most of the youngsters involved eventually apply to college, and many are admitted. More than 120 potential dropouts helped by Alice have gone to college and earned degrees.

Sweet Alice's pride and joy are the teenage mothers. Her philosophy: "Just because a young lady makes a mistake doesn't justify treating her like the lowest thing on the totem pole and making her ashamed." Alice builds the confidence of these girls and helps them find childcare and financial support so that they can return to school.

How do you explain Alice's ability to transcend her circumstances and use her lessons to help others? No one explains it better than she does: "The poor need help," she says, "and each of us has what they need. Whatever it is, even if it's just a smile, give it up. If you give back what God gave you, he'll give it back to you again. It's simple: the more you give, the more you receive."

Alice makes a genuine, astonishing difference in Watts because she has all that it takes—a heart full of kindness, love, and grace.

No political power or budget allotment could do what Alice has done in one of the most threatened neighborhoods in America. Only the seed of kindness, grown into full-blown, unstoppable love, explains the life of Alice Harris.

The Simplicity of Kindness

Saint Paul wrote a wonderful definition of kindness: ". . . be ye kind to one another, tenderhearted, forgiving one another . . . " (Eph. 4:32, KJV). Remember that our definition of Simplicity focuses on the ease of understanding a given concept, not the ease of following through in practice. Once we have understanding of the concept, the work of practicing becomes our task.

Let's focus, then, on those two words that describe the person who evidences kindness: *tenderhearted* and *forgiving*. Tenderheartedness is a quality of seeing another person's point of view, but doing so with gentleness and compassion. Native Americans have a saying that's survived to become a part of modern culture: "Don't judge a person until you've walked for a time in that person's moccasins." Such an attitude is the beginning of kindness. Taking the other person's point of view—trying to see his or her path, with its roots, rocks, and storms—is the first act of understanding that brings the individual out of a self-centered focus into an other-centered focus.

Forgiveness is also at the heart of what it means to relate to others with kindness. We all live with the tension that community brings: we need to be near one another and have relationships, yet that nearness invariably allows our natural selfishness to create misunderstanding and hurt. Forgiveness is the cleanser that removes those stains from relationships and allows relationships to grow and deepen. Forgiveness has to be a one-way street—in other words, I have to forgive you regardless of whether you in turn forgive me—and that kind of effort is terribly difficult for us.

Like most scriptural documents, the Bible illustrates these principles with real-life stories that teach great lessons. Forgiveness first became real for me when I discovered an ancient Bible story that deals with forgiveness in reverse—that is, what happens to a person who fails to forgive.

Most of us have heard of the biblical story of David, the boy who killed the giant Goliath and grew up to become king of the nation Israel. As king, he had many wise counselors who helped him win wars and administer a rapidly growing country. The wisest of these was a man named Ahithophel.

David made one great mistake in his life—a story detailed in 2 Samuel. He became infatuated with the wife of another man. Because David was king, he was able to assign the husband, Uriah, to the front lines during a battle. The man was killed, and David married the wife, Bathsheba, with whom he had already committed adultery.

The connection between these two things—the advice of Ahithophel and the adultery of David—is buried in a boring passage of scripture that records family history. In that passage the reader discovers that Ahithophel was the father of Bathsheba's father; in other words, he was Bathsheba's grandfather.

David later admitted his error and apologized. He provided for Uriah's family and treated Bathsheba very well. But the grandfather, Ahithophel, was angry. Unable to forgive, he harbored his anger until it became bitterness, rotting him from the inside out. Finally he joined a rebellion against David that resulted in a civil war.

Ahithophel's lack of forgiveness turned him from the wisest man in the nation into a vindictive, twisted person whose plans were no longer trusted. He went home in anger one day and committed suicide.

The person originally clearly in the wrong was David, while the person clearly in the right was Ahithophel. But Ahithophel had a hard heart; his unwillingness to change denied him the ability to forgive and ultimately resulted in his death. David's tender heart, on the other hand, led him to confess his sin and be forgiven by God. In the end, the child of his mistake became the greatest of all the kings of the ancient world, for Bathsheba was the mother of Solomon.

Kindness as an Inner Quality

To understand how the inner quality of kindness can be built into a powerful ability to love, we must approach the difficult issue of defining love. Novelists, songwriters, poets, and psychiatrists have attempted this task throughout history. Each attempt illuminates a beautiful facet; but love, like a perfect jewel, is always revealing another facet, always catching life's light in a new way.

Perhaps it would be better for me to try to clarify what love is *not*. One of the most damaging trends in U.S. society is the tendency to dethrone love from its position as the highest virtue in the universe by misrepresentation.

Contrary to popular culture, love isn't something you fall into, buy, make, or sell. One falls into a mud puddle. When we say "fall in love," we really mean "become infatuated." The intensity of infatuation never lasts, however; indeed, it would be too exhausting if it did. How many of us could function in life if we were continually swooning, dreaming, and forgoing food as we do when infatuated?

Sex isn't love either. You can "have sex," but if love doesn't surround the relationship, you can't "make love" in the bedroom. To put love in such terms devalues it unspeakably.

Nor can you buy or sell love. It's a gift that can only be freely given. The minute a price comes with a gift, it ceases to be a gift. Therefore, you can't love someone "because of " or "if." To say, "I love you because you make me feel happy," is to put a price on love and make it something else. I may like being around you because you make me happy, but I love you only when I decide to be around you no matter how you treat me.

Another amazing thing about love is that each generation must learn its lessons anew. Part of becoming fully human is wrestling with the great questions of life—love certainly ranks in that list—and growing by the struggle.

I've observed this phenomenon—this wrestling with the issue of love—in my three children. As an example, I watched my youngest, Jonathan, struggle with love when he was eight years old. Let me share that struggle.

My father began taking me out on overnight canoe trips when I was eight. Those trips were so special to me that I followed the tradition with each of my sons. When each one turned eight, we'd plan a trip for the next summer—a trip for just the two of us, a canoe, a tent, and the beautiful wilderness.

By the time Jonathan came along, I was really anticipating the trip. I had found with the older boys that such an outing afforded an opportunity for some very special moments. At least once during each of the earlier trips a situation or conversation had occurred that had brought us closer together.

Jon and I drove to a chain of lakes in the Adirondacks and launched our canoe. It was a bright but breezy day, and after about fifteen minutes of paddling into the wind, Jon said he needed a rest. Putting up his paddle, he soon arranged a comfortable perch out of our gear and leaned back facing me, apparently dozing in the sunshine.

I was considering waking him and asking for some assistance with the paddling when he opened one eye and said, "Dad, how old were you when you and Mom got married?"

"I was twenty-one, Jon," I replied. "Why do you ask?"

"I was just thinking: that doesn't give me much time."

Sensing that he was thinking deeply about this issue, and feeling that this might become one of those special moments, I fought down the urge to chuckle and replied seriously. "Well, Jon, you don't *have* to get married at twenty-one—and besides, that's thirteen years away. You haven't even lived thirteen years yet."

He pondered that for a while, trailing his fingers in the water beside the canoe. Finally he looked up and said, "Yeah, but Dad, how did you ever get such a beautiful woman like Mommy to marry *you?*"

Clearly he thought that the magnificent creature who was his mother was worthy of someone infinitely better than dumpy old Dad. I'd had enough of this conversation and was framing a blistering retort—perhaps pointing out that I was the one who arranged canoe trips (and indeed was doing all the work on this one) and didn't need sly put-downs from spoiled, bratty offspring. However, before I could get my thoughts organized and draw a breath, Jon answered his own question: "Well, I guess she just felt sorry for you!"

His eyes were full of amazement at the incredible fortune I had found. They were also full of doubt that he would ever be able to find someone as wonderful as his mother to do the same for him.

"Well, Jon," I said, "I don't think that your mother felt sorry for me, but you're right about one thing. She didn't marry me because of who I am but because of who she is. You see, loving is something you choose to do, and Mom chose to love me."

I'm not sure Jon got the lesson that day, but I sure did. Anyway, it satisfied him enough to get him paddling again.

Like faith and hope, love is a choice. It's a deeper choice than anything else, though. With faith, there's evidence to go on; with hope, there's expectation to inspire you forward. With pure love, there's nothing but your choice, for when any other qualification is introduced, the outcome ceases to be love.

The only proof of love is in loving. Only when you give love without regard to the getting do you find the true inner secret of love: love hoarded diminishes; love given multiplies.

Perhaps a simple definition will help clarify the concept. Like all definitions of love, it will necessarily be incomplete, but maybe it will reveal enough facets to show the incredible value of this jewel. Here is my simple definition: love is selfless concern for the best in the life of another.

"Selfless concern" means that you ignore your own wants and needs. Love can't be about how *you* feel or what *you* want; it must be about the other person. "Concern for the best" means a willingness to sacrifice not just in order that the object of your love is all right but in order that he or she thrives.

Transforming Your Kindness into Love

This brings us to the issue of the spiritual qualities of kindness that can be built into love. It's in these qualities that we'll find the greatest power in the universe for personal change. Saint Paul wrote that there are three everlasting and ever-powerful qualities: ". . . Faith, Hope, and Love. But the greatest of these is love" (1 Cor. 13:13).

Love is also the dividing factor in the world's great religions. Most religious groups fall into one of two categories. On the one hand are those that view God as a personal being who seeks a loving relationship with humankind. On the other hand are those who see God as an impersonal being or even a state of being that one must work to attain. In the first case, God comes down to us; in the second, we must climb to God.

Christianity, which falls into the first category, shapes my view of the world and our place in it. The famous British writer C. S. Lewis said that Christianity would better be called "Lovianity," because it was all about love. He took as his text this statement of Jesus from the Gospel of John: "For God so loved the world that he gave his one and only Son . . ." (3:16).

The definition of kindness given earlier in this chapter was from Saint Paul: "Be ye kind one to another, tenderhearted, forgiving one other." That passage from Ephesians goes on to say, ". . . even as God, for Christ's sake, has forgiven you." If you take the view that God is personal and is seeking to come to individuals, you can see that he begins with the kindness of forgiveness.

This is an incredibly freeing concept. Instead of a long list of Herculean tasks we must perform to attain spiritual perspective and power, we find that the first step is simply accepting kindness and forgiveness. Think of it this way: trying to get to God through our own efforts is sort of like trying to leap across the Royal Gorge in Colorado—a gorge that's more than a mile wide. I, being somewhat unathletic, might get ten feet from the side before failing and falling to the bottom of the gorge. You might be twice as strong and get twenty feet. Someone else might be twice again as good and get forty feet. However, no one would get all the way across. We'd all end up failing and falling.

Fortunately there's a bridge across the Royal Gorge. There's also a bridge to spiritual power: that bridge is God reaching out to us and saying, "Come on across; simply come to the bridge and step across." How foolish we would be to say, "No thanks, I'll try jumping."

Yet many people do just that in their spiritual lives. They keep trying harder and harder to love God instead of accepting the love God has already sent them. In so doing, they say, in effect, "No thanks, I'll keep jumping."

Believe me, I understand how difficult it is to accept this concept of God providing a bridge and demanding nothing more of us than that we accept his offer to walk across. I understand this difficulty because I've felt unconditional love, and it was hard to accept.

Eight weeks before Joy and I were to be married in 1975, I was in a terrible accident while traveling in Wisconsin. My condition was so critical that the doctors told Joy, who was in California, not to rush to Wisconsin. I wouldn't survive long, they said, and my body would be shipped home to Minnesota. She came anyway, traveling eighteen hours on three airplanes to get to Oshkosh.

When I regained consciousness after surgery, Joy's face was the first thing I saw. I learned later that the long flight, the little she'd eaten, and the shock of seeing me in such a condition had made her vomit when she first came into the room. The doctors urged her to leave, but she wouldn't. All that day, through the next day, and into the following morning she sat there. Serving in a small-town hospital, the staff allowed it, because—as the doctors later told me—I wasn't expected to live anyway.

After I'd survived for forty-eight hours, they decided maybe I had a chance after all. They also admitted that my vital signs showed an uptick every time my eyes opened and I saw Joy, so they continued to let her stay. Hour after hour she was there, reading to me, encouraging me.

Finally, after ten days, I was well enough to stand. That morning, before Joy came, I begged the nurse to let me use the bathroom. I was sick of bedpans. In defiance of policy, she let me push my IV tree into the bathroom, dragging tubes and wires along with me. Flipping on the light switch, I glanced at myself in the mirror—and started to scream.

The swollen features, jagged stitches, dried blood, and unkempt hair frightened me. I looked like a monster, even to myself. After calming down, I thought, "If I look this bad now, what was it like ten days ago when Joy arrived?" I couldn't imagine loving such a distorted creature and began to doubt that she should marry me. To her great credit, she never imagined calling off the wedding; and in the twenty years of our marriage, she's taught me even more about unconditional love.

Key Discoveries

Preparation

With this chapter we've completed the pieces necessary to construct a strong life pyramid. As shown below, from the foundations of Belief, Optimism, and Kindness we've built the framework of Faith, Hope, and Love.

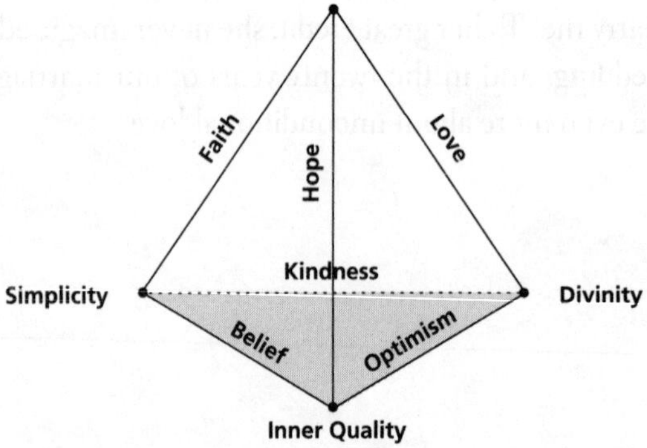

Kindness built into love is the most powerful force in the universe. By this force Gandhi threw off British colonial rule in India and Rosa Parks was joined by a nation of people, both black and white, in finally rejecting the injustice of segregation. What legislation and state troopers couldn't accomplish, compassion in the hearts of people who saw and heard Rosa did.

With these three foundational principles in your life, you have available to you one of the greatest tools for personal change ever discovered. Dr. Peale liked to call that tool the "as if " principle. You can begin today to act "as if " you had belief, as if you had optimism, as if you were filled with kindness. You'll find that once you begin acting "as if " you had a quality, that quality begins to appear in your life.

You can see that principle in action right here and now, if you're willing to risk trying the suggestions in the final section of each chapter. By one of life's most common paradoxes, you won't find them successful until you begin to use them.

Remember Sweet Alice? Until she stood up and began to help people, others weren't willing to help her. Yet she, by acting on her grounding principle before it was a reality in her life, proved that principle: "If you give to others what God gave to you, he'll give it back again."

The quickest way to gain compassion for others is to practice the Native American principle of walking a while in another person's moccasins. The next time a difficult person crosses your path, take the time to find out what influences in his or her life might be producing the harshness. Then take the time to reflect on how well you might handle similar circumstances. The results of that reflection can be both humbling and empowering.

Action

Take these three steps this week to multiply the presence of kindness in your life, thereby allowing true love to grow within you:

1. Clear the way for kindness by rooting out all bitterness. Remember the story of Ahithophel, the wise man who couldn't forgive and was driven to suicide. Don't let another person's unkindness or hateful spirit rule your life. Let go of the bitterness you're harboring before it eats you alive from the inside out.

2. Develop the three practices of kindness that form the basis of a loving life:

Tenderheartedness: Be willing to bend and absorb blows while maintaining inner strength.

Forgiveness: Forgive others for wrongs done; forgive yourself for past mistakes and move on.

Selflessness: Examine the closest love relationship you have. Can you honestly say that you're working for the best for that person without any regard to how he or she responds to you?

3. Take time to read and reflect on this scriptural passage, as paraphrased in the Living Bible:

Love is very patient and kind, never jealous or envious, never boastful or proud, never haughty or selfish or rude. Love does not demand its own way. It is not irritable or touchy. It does not hold grudges and will hardly even notice when others do it wrong.

"It is never glad about injustice, but rejoices whenever truth wins out. If you love someone you will be loyal to him no matter what the cost. You will always believe in him, always expect the best of him, and always stand your ground in defending him" (*I Cor. 13:4–7, LB*).

Chapter 6

Finding Your Spiritual Focal Point

Now that we've come to the halfway point in our journey through this book, it's time to draw together the threads we've been weaving and to look at the pattern they form. The starting place for that process could be called your "spiritual focal point."

Perhaps it would be helpful to remind ourselves of the definition of the word *spiritual*, as used in this book. We've said that *spiritual* is the word tied to the universal longing of people to find out about God. Religion, on the other hand, is someone's set of rules for that process. My purpose in this book is to get readers to begin their personal spiritual exploration. I'm confident that if you do so eagerly and honestly, God will come out to meet you, and that encounter will direct your religious practice.

Let's get specific about the matter of our spiritual existence. You'll notice that I haven't used the term "spiritual life" in my discussion. It's my belief that we've been done a great injustice by those who would segregate our thinking about ourselves into our "emotional life," our "physical life," our "mental life," and our "spiritual life." You and I have only *one* life; we coexist on several planes simultaneously within that life. Here's where the model of our life pyramid becomes important as a visual tool for understanding ourselves.

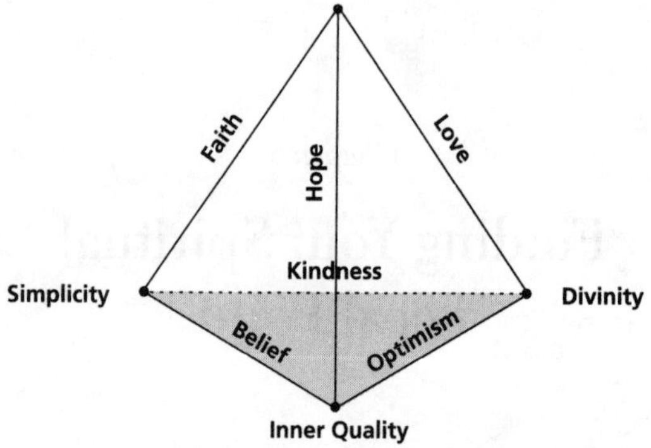

In the figure above you can see again how the foundational underpinnings of Belief, Optimism, and Kindness are built upward to complete the triangular pyramid. Belief builds up to become Faith. Optimism builds up to become Hope. Kindness builds up to become Love. If our pyramid didn't have a focal point, however, the structure might look like the one below, suggesting a life adrift, lacking both a defined purpose and the connectedness required to give the strength necessary to withstand the storms of life. All the pieces are there, but they're not assembled properly.

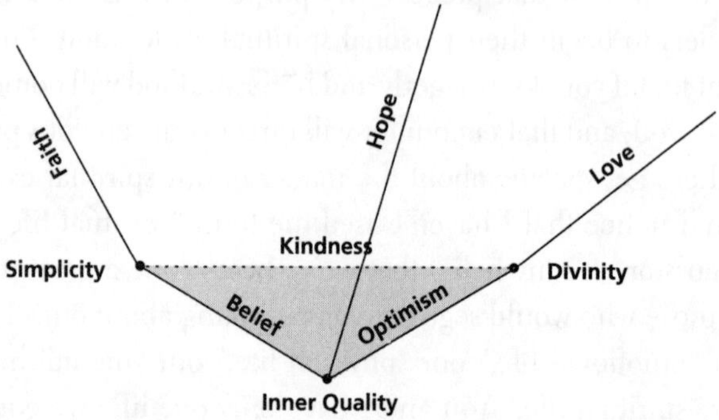

Similarly, you can place a point of focus above your life pyramid, but unless it's centered properly, even a "together" life will be out of balance. For instance, if you don't have a centered focus, the excessive growth of Optimism may pull Faith and Love out of shape, as shown below. You have a life that fits together, but it's out of balance.

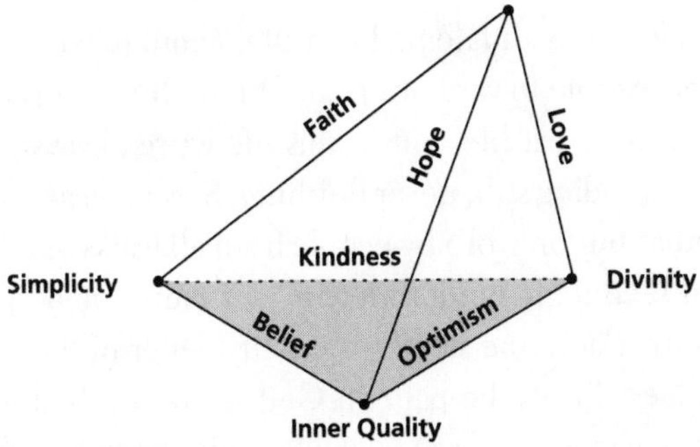

It's not my purpose here to describe all the various ways your life pyramid can be out of balance. Like all metaphors, the pyramid metaphor has its weaknesses. However, I'm sure that a trained psychologist or psychiatrist could give a name to the various out-of-balance configurations and give examples of life characteristics that indicate an unbalanced condition. Rather than get into these diagnostic discussions, let me propose a simple approach.

All of us are out of balance. People who have no spiritual focus are like the second pyramid above. The lines of their inner growth are loose, unconnected, and powerless. In extreme cases these people are given fancy labels, such as *neurotic* and *psychotic*, and they sometimes end up in prisons and hospitals. But even those of us who have pursued our spiritual potential and have identified a point of focus, tying in Faith, Hope, and Love, are out of balance to some degree. Unless we take the further step of examining and orienting our inner lives, that spiritual point can't be centered even temporarily.

Without that extra step, our internal lack of balance affects every area of our lives, yet that step is no guarantee of perfection. None of us ever achieves permanent, perfect balance in our inner lives. Life is about seeking and working toward that balance. Success is finding moments, days, weeks, months—yes, even years—when the balance is achieved, yet none of us stays in balance permanently in this life.

Life is a journey, and doing life well is about making as much progress as possible toward our goal. Our destination is a higher existence in the next life, but in this life we're always progressing—never standing still, never finishing. Several years ago there was a popular button worn by people from all walks of life. It displayed ten seemingly random letters that didn't spell anything: PBPGINFWMY. Each one stood for the first letter of the words in this sentence: "Please be patient; God is not finished with me yet." That slogan is the essence of what this chapter is all about.

Perhaps you're asking, "What difference does a spiritual focus make to my everyday life? What about the challenges I'm facing physically, emotionally, and mentally? *Those* are the things that drive me." In order to answer these not-unreasonable questions—that is, to understand the task and technique of gaining inner spiritual focus to balance your life pyramid—it might be helpful to look ahead.

Return for a moment to the life pyramid and let me add the final elements, those that are the focus of the second half of this book. Let's assume a perfectly balanced triangular pyramid, as shown in the figure below.

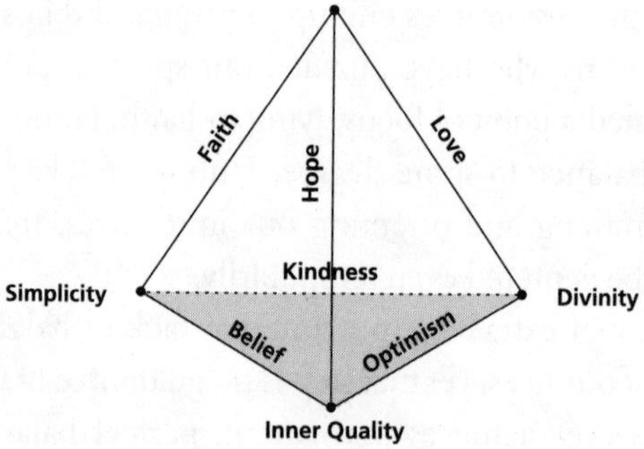

This is the framework of the balanced life. It's the structure that holds all the other elements of life together. Now, to carry the picture forward, fill in the three empty planes that form the sides of this pyramid with "wall panels" that represent your physical, emotional, and mental facets, as the next figure illustrates. As you can see, if the inner framework is out of balance, your three outward facets—physical, emotional, and mental (or body, soul, and mind)—are pulled into an unbalanced condition.

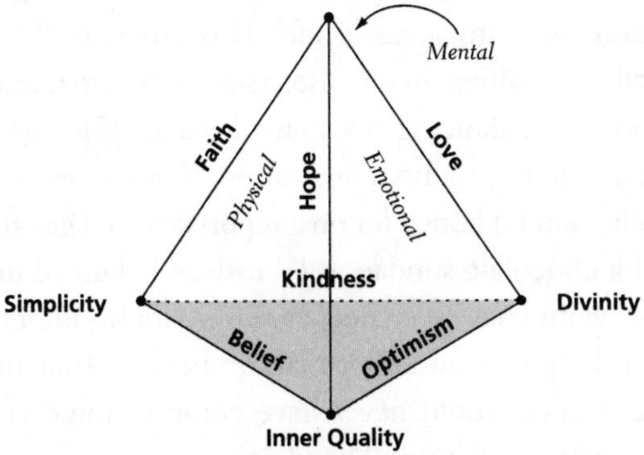

Now you have a nearly complete picture of a balanced life pyramid. All that remains is a discussion about the plane represented by the base, and we'll take that up later. The fleshed-out picture in the above figure illustrates the concept, touched on earlier, that you have only one life. That life contains many elements, but it's nonetheless a *singular* unity, as represented by the pyramid.

This picture also focuses on the importance of the framework in keeping the outer elements of life in balance. Permit me a simple personal example. I'm about twenty-five pounds overweight. There are only two possible fundamental reasons for that condition. The first possibility is that outside forces beyond my control are responsible. In that case I must absorb this negative physical condition by keeping the rest of life in such good balance that the bad side effects of the extra weight are minimized. The second possibility is that some part of my inner framework is out of balance, pulling my physical plane out of shape too.

Admittedly, the latter is true for me. I'm overweight because I overeat. I overeat because my capacity for hope is expansive, not held in check by equal amounts of love and faith.

"What?" you say. "Give me a break!" Just bear with me for a minute. Think back. Hope produces expectations. Hope not balanced produces unreasonably high expectations, leading to unfulfilled dreams in many areas of life. This produces the stress of dissatisfaction, resulting, in my case, in overeating to reduce stress.

In short, not balancing my natural capacity for extra hope with love and faith produces overeating. If one of my sons got a lower grade than I'd hoped for on a report card, I'd get angry and fix myself a chocolate sundae. If I'd instead balanced that hope with love, I would have seen deeper reasons for his low grade and focused on helping him rather than on my dissatisfaction. The chocolate sundae would never have come to mind (let alone found its way to my waistline) had I done so.

Life works from the inside out. Many times I've gone through scenarios similar to the simple one described above and essentially ended up blaming my son for my overeating. Oh, I never shouted, "I wouldn't be stuffing all this ice cream down my throat if it weren't for your report card," but I did console myself with the ice cream. I did tell myself I "deserved" it. After all, how could anyone be asked to cope with such blatantly unrealized potential? Better to eat ice cream than to kick the dog.

Do you see what I was doing? I was blaming my choice to overeat on outside circumstances even though I'm in control of how much I eat and what it does to my waistline. (That's not always the case, however. In some people overeating is caused by a chemical imbalance or some other outside force.)

We'll explore these dynamics more fully and consider ideas for finding and keeping your spiritual balance in the next few chapters. For now, though, let's return to finding a spiritual focus that allows our inner framework to be in balance, thereby balancing the outer elements of life.

The metaphor and diagrams of the life pyramid point out the importance of a spiritual focal point. As we've seen, the elements of your inner framework need to be connected at one point in order for them to lean on one another and provide the strength needed for a happy and successful life.

Here again we see why it's so important to throw off the old idea of having several "lives" that you move between. Although people talk colloquially about their physical, mental, emotional, and love lives, you have only one life. All those various elements are present, to be sure; but they're present at the same time, and each is affected by the condition of the others.

Spirituality isn't on a par with these elements, however; it's not just another element of the framework or plane on the outer life. It's more than part of the building; it's the reference point by which all else in the building is measured and aligned. For too long in the United States we've tended to ignore the importance of spiritual focus. That's like trying to build a house by starting on all sides of the foundation at once, without setting the cornerstones in place.

Recently, fascinating stories focusing on these questions have appeared in the secular press. The February 1995 issue of *Industry Week* magazine displayed the cover headline "Give Us That Old-Time Religion." The related articles proposed that spiritual values were the real need in the modern factory, in order to increase productivity and worker quality of life.

The October 1995 issue of *Atlantic Monthly* devoted its cover to the question, "If the Economy Is Up, Why Is America Down?"

A lengthy article explored the question of why people feel so bad about their future when all leading economic indicators are up. Several symptoms were listed: "People were working longer hours for less pay, . . . commutes were more harried. Crime, congestion, and media violence were increasing. More families were falling apart. A *Business Week*/Harris poll in March 1995 imparted the not surprising news that more than 70 percent of the public was gloomy about the future."

The *Atlantic* article goes on to show how the current calculation of our gross domestic product (GDP) actually measures negative cultural influences as economic progress. The article described former education secretary William Bennett's Index of Leading Cultural Indicators as an index of "crime, divorce, [and] mass media addiction" and noted that those factors actually add to the GDP.

For instance, divorce positively impacts the real estate market, because when a single family unit breaks into two or more parts, each needs housing. And billions of dollars are spent on theft- and crime-deterrent products not needed ten years ago, raising the GDP. But how can those things be called progress? Surely some measure of a nation's spiritual health is needed to balance its economic performance.

Take this concept from the national scene into the personal one. What does success mean if you're a miserable person? And if that's your condition, how can you get out of the misery? A look at the three areas that support our spiritual framework provides part of the answer.

The Framework of Faith

Finding a spiritual focus begins with Faith. When Saint Paul wrote, "And now these three remain: Faith, Hope, and Love," he was describing the logical progression that Faith leads to Hope and Hope leads to Love. Success without Faith is meaningless and often personally debilitating.

Actress Rene Russo grew up in a tough part of Burbank, California. She quit school at seventeen to work in an eyeglass company. One day an agent for a modeling agency saw her at a concert and invited her to New York to try modeling. Soon she was in the pages of all the top fashion magazines, and her life became what many would describe as successful.

In a December 3, 1995, interview in *Parade* magazine, Russo recalls, "The big thing I got out of [modeling] was going from having very little money to suddenly getting whatever I wanted. I was able to buy myself a house. I bought my Mom a house. I bought a Porsche. But you know what? I was still miserable.

"I started out thinking, 'Gee, I'd like to get a cover.' Then you get a cover, and you think, 'If I only could get *two* covers.' Then that happens, and it's still not enough. You want to be *the* top model. All those things I thought would bring me happiness I reached really fast, and none of it worked for me.

"For one thing, I never bought into other people's idea of me. Here the industry is saying you're beautiful, and I really wanted to believe it. But I was so caught up in having *them* like me that I was never able to feel good about me myself.

"So the money didn't do it. And the attention didn't do it. It seemed like I had a different boyfriend every two and a half years. I always found myself sort of joyless. I did my job almost like a robot and, as quickly as I could, went home to where I felt safe."

Finally a friend saw her turmoil and suggested that she try to get help. Rene thought, "My God, how can he see that in me? Am I really that transparent?

"I took off four years and studied theology. I went to my church, where they give classes. Quite frankly, it's the best thing

I've ever done. It taught me what I'd been looking for. I learned that faith was what I needed to give me the self-esteem I didn't have. Faith is knowing that I've been put on this earth with certain gifts and certain goals and that I'm going to end up where I'm supposed to—no matter what I'm going through right now. When you have faith, you can't help but accept yourself."

External success continued with Rene. She starred in the hit movie *Major League* and went on to act alongside some of Hollywood's biggest leading men, including Mel Gibson, Clint Eastwood, and Dustin Hoffman. She has a good marriage and a beautiful daughter, Rose.

"I'm not saying life is not a struggle anymore," Rene said. "It always will be. . . . Do I get up some days and feel competitive? Sure. Do I get up some days and feel afraid? Of course. But what's different is that I'm different. The way I feel about myself today is so different than even five years ago that it's exciting. I have real moments of joy now, and I know it will continue."

Listen to the message in Rene's story. Her circumstances haven't changed; she has. Now she *overcomes* her circumstances. And she knows life is a journey. She isn't looking for unending joy; she knows joy comes in moments. But when your life has begun coming into focus through faith, you can count on those moments of joy more and more frequently.

The Framework of Hope

We've defined Hope as the expectation of divine assistance for success. A simpler, day-by-day definition might be "positive expectation." When you take these two ideas together—positive expectation and an awareness of the divine order of things—your vision changes. This change is the key to seeing life in such a way that you begin finding all the possibilities, even in the middle of problems. That expanded vision is at the heart of making life work.

As I sit at my study window, I see a large puddle covering the far corner of our front yard. Once this annual spring occurrence bothered me greatly. I would rush out and clear the leaves and sticks from the rocks that were supposed to allow this overflow to drain away. Each summer I would build a high bank of earth to hold back the rain-swollen tide that I knew would eventually crest, and each spring my efforts would fail.

Then, several years ago, I woke one Saturday to find the front yard a virtual lake. The puddle had grown overnight to the point where miniature waves lapped along the edge of the driveway. Discouragement crept over me as I thought of all the past summer's hard work, now washed away. My son Nathan, then eight, was sitting beside me as I sipped my morning coffee. Suddenly, with wonder in his eyes, Jonathan, then six, burst in and shouted, "Look, Dad! God made a lake in our front yard! Hurry, get the canoe."

As he ran out to get his paddle and life vest, I heaved a deep sigh. Hearing me, Nathan gave me his wisest look and said, "You've got to understand, Dad: to a third-grader like me it's just a big puddle, but to a first-grader it's a miracle."

That lake has come back almost every spring since. Yet now I see it though Jon's eyes of wonder, and it becomes a shimmering sea to explore and a raging river to navigate. It's the same messy puddle, of course; only my view has changed. Besides, if I wait until July, as I've learned to do, it always dries up!

The exercise of hope, in union with an awareness of God's presence all around, draws life into a closer spiritual focus and enables us to see the upside in every down situation, thereby enabling us to work our way through until the downside is behind us.

The Framework of Love

Saint Paul said, "And now these three remain: Faith, Hope, and Love. But the greatest of these is Love." In the same way that seeking faith allows hope to grow, hope-filled living produces fertile ground for deep and abiding love. This isn't the love portrayed in popular entertainment. It's the real thing, containing both passion and pain.

In his book *Love Is a Feeling to Be Learned*, writer Walter Trobisch gives the best description of real love that I've seen outside Saint Paul: "Love is a feeling to be learned. It is deep longing and fulfillment. It is gladness and it is pain. There is not one without the other. Happiness is only a part of love—this is what has to be learned. Suffering belongs to love also. This is the mystery of love, its beauty and its burden. Love is a feeling to be learned."

In 1983 I visited mainland China during the first year that Westerners were allowed to move somewhat freely around the country. My deep spiritual interest led me to examine and write about the recent reopening of certain churches, both Catholic and Protestant—churches that hadn't been allowed to function since the 1960s. My guide was a Chinese-American student who spoke the language well and had traveled "in country" before.

One afternoon north of Shanghai he asked if I would be willing to take on a little danger. We left the group bus—an action that was frowned upon—and traveled for two hours by truck and then foot. As we approached the top of a rather desolate hill, my guide told me to stop walking and crawl the last few yards to the summit, being careful to remain out of sight, especially if I saw anyone below.

As we lifted our heads and looked down the other side, I saw what at first appeared to be a factory. A couple of four- or five-story buildings made up the compound, and I could see people moving back and forth across the grounds. I noticed pieces of heavy equipment and saw many people pushing wheelbarrows and carts. Then I noticed a fence around the entire area, with what appeared to be guards stationed at regular intervals along the perimeter.

"What is this place?" I asked.

"It's a prison," came the reply. "I thought you would be interested, because this is where all the religious leaders are kept, whether Hindu, Buddhist, Protestant, or Catholic.

"You see, the church buildings are being allowed open again, but many of these prisoners will never get out."

"How long have they been here?" I asked.

"Most of them since the so-called Cultural Revolution began in 1960," he replied. "Religious leaders were among the first people rounded up, condemned for antigovernment beliefs. The bureaucracy is such that even though the government has changed its mind, it will take years to hear all these cases."

It was a sobering statement about freedom of spiritual expression, one I carry with me still. But that conversation wasn't the end of that particular story.

A couple of weeks later we left China and traveled to Hong Kong, where I was to spend a few days before returning home. While we were there, my student friend asked if I would like to visit some friends of his in their home. Anxious to get past the hotel district and see what Hong Kong was really like, I readily agreed.

So it came about that we trekked into the vast honeycomb of local streets that make up most of Hong Kong. One of the most crowded cities on the planet, its sights and smells aren't always familiar (or pleasant) to Westerners. Finally we arrived at the apartment building and walked up the three flights to the home of his friends.

They were an older couple, probably in their late fifties at the time, and spoke no English. Clearly they were expecting us and had prepared for me as an honored guest. While we were seated on their sofa and the woman was preparing tea, I began to notice an unusual interaction between this couple. They were, to the best of my Western understanding, flirting with each other. Gentle touches of fingers to cheeks, sparkling eyes following each other's movements, and a certain musical chuckle spelled romance in any language.

I must have been staring, because soon they were laughing and pointing to me. When I asked my student friend what was so funny, he replied, "You are! Why are you staring at them?"

"Well," I stammered, "it does seem unusual to see such behavior in an older couple, especially when they're Chinese and I'm American. Most of the Chinese we've met are very formal around strangers."

"Oh," he replied, "but you're with me, so you're not a stranger. Besides, although they're old friends, they're newlyweds."

The twinkle in his eye told me I'd been set up, so I asked how come they'd waited so long to marry since they were so obviously in love. My new friends, whom I'll call Mr. and Mrs. Shen, told the following story.

On a Friday in 1960 they were together in the chapel at Nanging Seminary rehearsing for their wedding, which was to take place the next day. Through the back door burst soldiers of the Red Guard, who hauled all the men off, including Mr. Shen, because they were seminary students. After a cold and frightening night, they were called in one by one to the commander's office. When Shen's turn came, he was given a document to sign—a document containing a lengthy statement about the foolishness of religion and concluding with a sworn statement that he would forever forsake the faith and would never practice it again.

When he politely declined to sign the statement, an order was given and his fiancée was dragged crying into the room. "Sign the statement now, Shen," said the commander, "and you can go home and be married tonight, just as you'd planned. Refuse to sign, and you'll never see your bride again."

Choked with tears, Shen whispered, "I cannot do as you ask."

The next day Shen was taken far away to the prison I had visited. One year later, to the day, he was called into the prison warden's office. When he came into the waiting room, there was his fiancée. They called out to each other but weren't allowed to be together. Inside, the warden placed the same document before him and said, "Sign this and go home, Shen; you've suffered enough. Sign now and go home to your bride."

Quietly he replied, "I cannot do as you ask."

When he was taken out, the waiting room was empty.

For fourteen more years the same pattern was repeated. Each year the quiet refusal brought another year of backbreaking labor in the prison factory. Finally, in the sixteenth year, his fiancée wasn't there when he came to the office. "See what a fool you've been," said the warden. "Even your intended bride has given up on you. Sign the document now and go home, you fool."

With quiet dignity and a broken heart, Shen again refused. He had no way of knowing that his fiancée had escaped to Hong Kong and was working twelve-hour days to earn enough money to bribe his release. It took her seven years, during which he continued to labor in the prison factory. One day a guard, acting at Shen's fiancée's behest, smuggled him out and hid him on a freighter bound for Hong Kong. When the ship docked at the pier, there was his beloved fiancée! Just two weeks prior to my visit, they had been married.

When I asked how he could possibly have lasted all that time, his reply began with one word: "Love. We loved one another and had dedicated our lives to the church. My friend, don't you know that Jesus loved me enough to die for me? How could I possibly forsake my faith?"

By now I was the one with tears. Never before or since have I seen such a shining example of the power of love that had found its spiritual source.

Each of the inner elements of life—faith, hope, and love—is strengthened and connected by spiritual focus. That focus is not necessarily found by looking for spirituality apart from your inner development. Rather, it is found as you look for spirituality through your inner development of faith, hope, and love. When you seek faith genuinely, opening yourself up to the God-question within, then Faith grows upward toward its natural spirituality. The same is true for Hope and Love. Eventually, as you continue the process, the honest seeking you do causes those lines of the life pyramid to intersect, locating your spiritual center.

Key Discoveries

Preparation

Throughout this chapter we've explored the importance of a spiritual focal point to join together the elements of Faith, Hope, and Love that develop in your inner life. This creates a triangular pyramid that forms the framework that holds the physical, mental, and emotional elements of your life in balance. Unless the framework is properly constructed and tied to a focused spiritual center, the pyramid is out of shape and distorts the other elements of life.

All of us are out of shape to some degree. Life is about building our framework of Faith, Hope, and Love and finding the spiritual focus that holds those elements in balance. Once the framework and focus are in place, then we go about centering the focus in order to bring life into balance. It's a dynamic process that's never finished and never completely sustained. This knowledge frees us from the guilt of not being perfect and allows us to enjoy the journey of discovery.

Action

The first step in finding your spiritual focus is believing in, or at least suspending your disbelief of, the presence and power of the spiritual nature of the universe. In my view God is present all around us. As you open yourself to that reality and those thoughts, you open yourself for God to become present within you. Once this process is begun, your spiritual awareness becomes the guiding force in the extension of your Faith, Hope, and Love.

Extending the framework of Faith, Hope, and Love from the seeds of Belief, Optimism, and Kindness gives shape, substance, and strength to your life pyramid. That framework then becomes the strength behind the development and maximization of your mental, physical, and emotional sides.

Extending Faith, Hope, and Love begins with a clear spiritual focus, but there are practical steps we can take for each piece of the frame. Faith is often built most readily by reading and thinking, Hope is generally given shape and form through writing, while Love becomes real through action.

FAITH

"Faith cometh by hearing and hearing by the Word of God," wrote Saint Paul in his epistle to the Romans 10:17 (KJV). Find a spiritual teacher who interests you and listen to his or her audiotapes while driving, walking, exercising, or preparing for sleep. Obviously my favorite is Norman Vincent Peale. If you write to me at the Peale Center, I'll be happy to send you a list of his materials that are available.

Read something spiritual every day. My favorite source is the Bible. I like the Psalms, Proverbs, and the writings of the apostles John and Paul. For contemporary writers, you might check out Max Lucado, Charles Swindoll, and Paula D'Arcy, along with Dr. Peale.

HOPE

Hope is nurtured largely through writing. Victor Frankl and Corrie Ten Boom survived the Nazi death camps partly by writing out their thoughts on scraps of paper and in their minds; they were building hope. I build hope largely through goal setting.

Someone once said that a goal is a dream with a deadline. Take this book, for example. For about six years I thought about writing it, talked about writing it, even started collecting notes and thoughts in files to organize writing it. But I didn't start actually writing it until a friend in the publishing business promised to take the idea to a publisher if I would keep a deadline and get some words down.

In order to be powerful, a goal must be (1) written, (2) measurable, and (3) challenging and attainable.

Kenneth Blanchard, author of *The One-Minute Manager* (and a friend and mentor), says that goals must be SMART, an acronym that breaks down as follows:

Specific: Don't just say, "I want to improve this year." Be specific about what you want to improve.

Motivational: A goal won't be very exciting unless you create some way to make it exciting. Be sure to reward yourself for achieving the goal.

Attainable: Don't set a goal so difficult that you'll never get there.

Relevant: Zero in on key goals that will make the biggest impact.

Trackable: Set up a score-keeping system (using checkpoints or some other means) to measure attainment.

Keep a notebook of your hopes and dreams and then put a deadline to some of those dreams by turning them into goals.

LOVE

Walter Trobisch wrote that "love is emotion in motion." In order to grow love, you must give it away. The only way to receive true love is to first give it. Just as water is the only physical element that expands when frozen, love is the only spiritual element that increases when you give it away.

Love is action. Thinking about love isn't the same as living out love. Remember the saying, "Actions speak louder than words." Set some time aside to read to a child, visit a nursing home, or write a letter to that sibling you've been fighting with. If you're a man and married, dedicate thirty minutes each night this week to talking to your wife. If you're a woman, choose a day this week to meet your husband at the door with his fishing pole, golf clubs, or basketball tickets. Send him off guilt-free to enjoy a favorite activity that you don't enjoy.

PART TWO

Using Your Spiritual Framework to Maximize the Mental, Emotional, and Physical Elements of Your Life

In this next section we'll explore how the inner spiritual framework of our life pyramid strengthens and holds in balance the mental, physical, and emotional elements of life.

Using the three-dimensional triangular pyramid as our model, we'll work in this next section to add the panels of our mental, physical, and emotional being to the framework of Faith, Hope, and Love.

This raises another question about our development that I want to acknowledge but not explore fully. To do so would require another book.

Look at the following model. It's obvious that there are three spaces available in the frame for the three aspects of being: mental, physical, and emotional. The question is, Where do you put which frame? For instance, do you put your physical being in the space framed at the top by Faith/Love, in the space framed by Love/Hope, or in the space framed by Hope/Faith? For purposes of this book, it doesn't matter. In your own life, however, it matters a great deal as you seek out your unique personhood. Each one of us has the same framework, but the arrangement of our being is different. You share a combination with other people, and psychology professors would call that combination your "personality type."

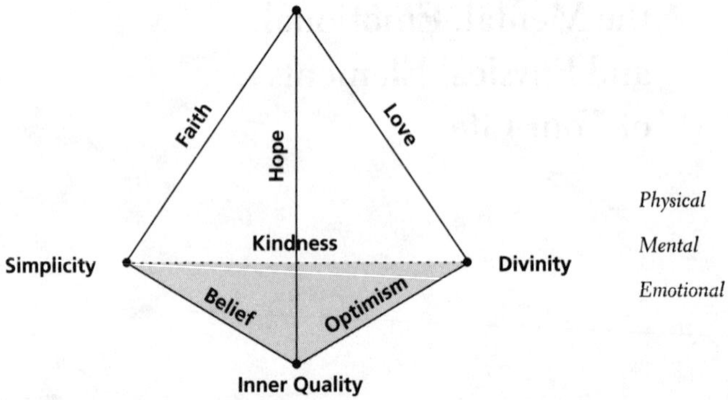

The framing elements (Faith, Hope, and Love) are joined at the top—at your spiritual focal point—because they all have a part in shaping your three elements of being (mental, physical, and emotional). In other words, all elements of being are guided by your spirituality.

In this section we'll explore how faith, hope, and love, guided by your spirituality, can be used to maximize your mental, physical, and emotional being.

Chapter 7

Using Your Spiritual Framework to Strengthen Your Mental Being

One of the people who inspired Norman Vincent Peale was the father of modern psychology, William James. Early in the 1900s James, a psychologist and philosopher, wrote, "The greatest discovery of my generation is that human beings can alter their lives by altering their attitudes of mind."

His was the generation that discovered the internal combustion engine, the automobile, the airplane, the telephone, radio communication, and practical uses for electricity. Yet James felt that all these inventions were minuscule in light of the realization that the mind is the most powerful tool humans possess. Why?

Throughout history, the power of ideas has overcome the forces of technology, education, and even (to some extent) nature. New ideas that challenge the old order have often been seen as bigger threats than armies. When Galileo proposed that the sun didn't revolve around the earth, he was thrown in jail. Why? Given the close relationship between the church and government in those days, the rulers couldn't afford to have people question the church's earth-centered theology. If people no longer believed that the earth was the center of the universe—the focus of God's attention—governmental authority and power would be undermined. Long before Galileo's theory came to wide attention, this threat was recognized, and the attempt to squelch him was immediate.

And what happened? Before Galileo's death, his ideas had begun to filter into the scientific community and were well on their way to permeating the entire world. He was a "powerless" individual, completely at the mercy of both the church and the government. Yet his ideas, based in reality and communicated simply, couldn't be held back. No decree, no punishment, no police force could stop their almost spontaneous spread.

Despots and dictators know this truth. Throughout history, from ancient times to Queen Mary to Hitler to Saddam Hussein, books have been burned, radio and television controlled, intellectuals jailed and murdered. Even the printing press, invented in the 1400s, was seen as such a threat that its inventor, Gutenberg, had to flee his native home and print copies of the Bible in a foreign country.

Ideas are also very powerful on a personal level. A life can literally be changed by them.

One of the greatest examples of this principle I've ever seen occurred in the life of a merchant seaman. As a young man Tom Riles dreamed of a life at sea. Growing up in New Jersey, he had an easy drive to the ocean. Tom went not just to the nearby beach to enjoy the look and smell of the surf but to the great harbors to gaze out at the ships coming and going and to marvel at the cargoes that came from around the world. He set his mind on being a sailor.

After completing high school, Tom pursued his dream. He attended Massachusetts Maritime Academy and became a Merchant Marine officer. Still he wanted more. He began to dream of becoming a harbor pilot. With nothing to support his dream but his own thinking, Tom began to study. There were courses to take, there was experience to gather, but his study had a practical goal: a harbor pilot's license.

Soon the power of the idea was propelling Tom toward his goal. Did it happen overnight? No. But did Tom take a step each day that gained ground toward his goal, and could he look back after a few years and see how far he'd come? Yes.

Then, just a few months before he was scheduled to take his examination, something happened to change Tom's thinking. Tragedy entered his life and hit Tom hard. His brother, Verne, with whom he had always been close, was in a car accident that left him in a coma due to brain injury. Tom and his family learned to live one day at a time, hoping and praying for the best. After four months in a coma, Verne died.

Devastated by Verne's death, Tom lost focus and abandoned his plans to take his harbor pilot's exam. His brother's tragedy left Tom unable to think of being away from his family, so he stayed on land. After six months his Merchant Marine officer's license lapsed.

The grief and pain blocked Tom's thoughts until he could hardly function. For six long years he was dragged down by memories of the death. He lost one job after another, finally becoming nearly destitute. His family could only sit by and watch what appeared to be total self-destruction.

One day, after a spell out of work, Tom applied for a menial part-time, temporary job. "It was a job washing bubble gum off the sidewalk in front of a large store in the downtown area," Tom recalls. "Even at my low point I was sure that I would get the job, because it called for so much less than my skills as a seaman. But I didn't get the job."

Angry, hurt, and at the end of his rope, Tom went back to ask the manager why he hadn't gotten the job. "He told me it was only one thing: the man they gave the job to had a better attitude."

Tom was jolted into reflection. "That simple statement crushed me," he says. "If I couldn't even get a job washing bubble gum off a sidewalk, how could I go on? I kept thinking over and over about how my attitude had lost me this last-chance opportunity. There seemed only one choice: I had to change my attitude.

"The following morning I woke up at five and started a routine I still follow today. After I take a two-mile brisk walk, I read the Bible for half an hour. Then I list with pen and paper all of the things I have to be thankful for on that day. Years ago someone gave me an old copy of *The Power of Positive Thinking* by Dr. Peale. The cover of the book had this statement: *Read this book and change your life*. That sounded good to me, because I *needed* a change. I started keeping a daily journal and applying positive thinking to all I did, especially writing out daily goals."

The change was dramatic. Within a few months Tom had gone from a listless person with no confidence to a telephone sales rep who had to exude the ultimate in confidence. Soon his productivity brought him to the attention of the company president, and he was given greater responsibility. By the time I met Tom in 1993, he had brought in over a million dollars of sales for his company.

The story doesn't end with material success, however. When he saw the dramatic change in his own life, Tom began to think of how his story could help others—especially young people. He wondered how many of the disadvantaged youth in his area could do the same thing he had done.

"Not many people have been as desperate as I was when out of work and trying for a job washing sidewalks," said Tom. "I knew that if I could get kids to see other possibilities, they could do a lot more with their lives than they thought they could."

So, while supporting his family and working his job, Tom started the Empathy Foundation and the Positive Kids program. With a goal of building bridges between urban and suburban youth, Tom organized several New Jersey townships in programs involving schoolchildren with helping the homeless. One effort in November 1995 delivered blankets from third- and fourth-graders. A second effort taught children about the challenges blind people face and raised funds to purchase and train a seeing-eye dog for a blind young person.

From sidewalk-washing failure to foundation coordinator, Tom Riles changed his life when he changed his thinking.

Most of us have heard the clichés "Thoughts are things" and "Nothing can stand in the way of an idea whose time has come." A writer I know, Gerald Mann, says ideas that stay around long enough to become corny do so because they're both simple and nutritious. That means they stick in your mind and carry life-changing truths.

Learning to think differently *can* change your life. The Bible teaches this principle in Proverbs 23:7: "For as he thinketh in his heart, so is he." (KJV) Not being a psychiatrist, I have no theories to explain why this is true, but I can tell you, having observing the changed lives of thousands of people, how it works.

Your actions and choices in life are controlled by responses generated in your brain. Think of your brain as something dynamic and moldable, like a piece of living clay. A single thought strokes gently over the soft clay. The same thought, repeated often enough, causes a groove to appear in the clay. That groove is an attitude. If the thought continues to recur, that groove—that attitude—becomes deeply ingrained and habitual. If an attitude is negative or hurtful, it can be removed through the effort of generating opposite thoughts that push the clay in a different direction, creating a groove that gives new attitudes a place to run. Those new attitudes create new behaviors and produce real and lasting change.

Sound too simple? Remember, I promised that *everything* in this book would be simple. Simplicity is exactly the reason many people don't try to change themselves. But they're confusing Simplicity with ease. "All I have to do is change my thinking?" they ask. "That's too easy." And they proceed to ignore thought-change and thereby do nothing. Changing your thoughts, while simple, is *not* easy. Allow me a personal example.

Several years ago the transition from college life to office work began to add pounds to my weight and inches to my waistline. Over time, spending my days behind a desk and neglecting daily sports practice took the expected toll. Soon I was adding about five pounds a year. The necessity of getting a new wardrobe made me evaluate the situation.

For me, dieting wasn't an option. Because I travel and eat out a lot in my work, I knew I would find it impossible to stick to a calorie-counting regime. However, I *could* fit exercise into my life. All the books and articles I'd seen said that moderate exercise could add years to my life and get the weight gain under control. "Twenty minutes three times a week" was the mantra.

Simple. But not easy. Deciding I needed equipment, I spent several hundred dollars on a cross-country ski machine. Joy, wanting to be an encouragement, joined me in trying it out. I lasted two days; Joy, who didn't need exercise for the same reasons I did, kept at it. Every morning I'd linger in bed, offering all kinds of reasons why that day wouldn't be one of my three times a week. Joy, on the other hand, would get right up, go downstairs, and use the machine. "You just have to decide you're going to do it," she told me firmly.

Fine. But how? How could I change my thinking from making excuses into making changes? One day, standing in front of the mirror knotting my tie, I couldn't help but notice the bulge straining over my belt (which was already at the last notch). Disgusted, I asked myself, "Do you want to look like this the rest of your life?" Somehow that question stuck. From then on, when

I'd start to roll over for another thirty-minute snooze, the image in the mirror would repeat, "Do you want to look like this?"

First I started with every Monday, promising myself to hit Wednesday and Friday if possible. When that didn't work as well as I'd hoped, I told myself to do three days in a row and get it over with. That worked. Soon I was exercising not just three days, but four or five. I felt and slept better, and life's tough events seemed less daunting.

One day, on a trip, I found myself looking around the motel for an exercise room. I was actually disappointed when none was available! It hit me then how much I had changed in two years. For fifteen years I'd never thought of exercising while traveling. Now I won't stay anywhere that doesn't provide that opportunity. A new habit—a very good habit—had started with a change in my thinking.

So you get the idea: changing your thinking can change your life. How does all this fit in with the life pyramid we're constructing? What does it have to do with developing our spiritual potential? Let's go back to our model for an answer.

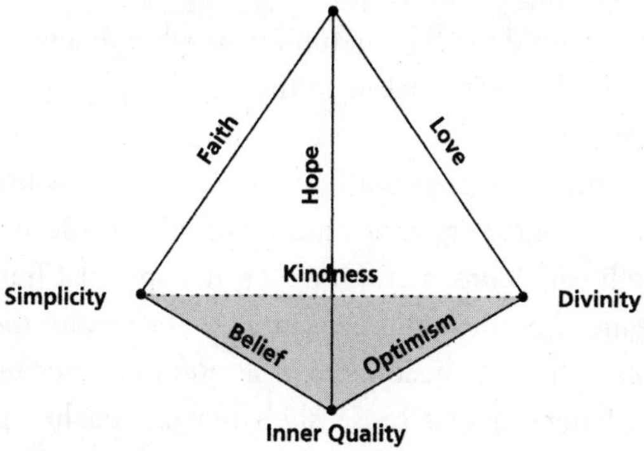

In previous chapters I've described how the inner qualities of Faith, Hope, and Love form the framework upon which the rest of our life is built. By thinking of the pyramid in three dimensions, we can see how that spiritual framework holds together the practical (or outer) planes of our existence: our mental, emotional, and physical being, as represented by the three vertical planes of the pyramid. The various ways in which these three planes are supported by the inner framework create the many different personality types we observe in each other.

For instance, your mental plane may be best defined (that is, framed at the sides) by Hope and Faith, as in the previous example. Yet, as you can see, the support of Love comes up behind the plane framed by Faith and Hope. If Love were not there, the plane would fall down. In short, each part of our inner framework—Faith, Hope, and Love—must be in balance, or our outer planes—mental, emotional, and physical—will be out of balance or distorted in shape.

No model, including our life pyramid, is accurate in every detail, because we're living, dynamic creatures with infinite possibilities and abundant creativity. Yet such a model is often useful in helping us focus our thinking and pursue goals that, once modeled, are simple in concept.

The life pyramid model is helpful in another practical aspect: it can help us deal with factors in life that are beyond our control—factors that seem to distort our outer planes despite the strength of our inner spiritual framework. If a girl is born with cerebral palsy, for example, no amount of spiritual development and strength can "cure" her. However, her spiritual framework can so balance her life—compensating, as it were, for the physical difficulty—that she becomes a profound influence on everyone around her. In that sense she's maximized her physical potential; it's in balance because it's serving her life purpose.

M. Scott Peck is famous for his wonderful book *The Road Less Traveled,* a roadmap for personal spiritual journeys. Yet one of his lesser-known works, a novel titled *A Bed by the Window*, deeply affected me as well. That novel illustrates this point of balance in spite of seeming deformity.

One of the main characters in the book is Stephen, a young man born with a severe spastic condition. He's unable to move much of his body, feed himself, or talk. He's highly intelligent, however, and communicates by tapping out letters on a board with his gnarled fingers. Of all the patients in the nursing home (the setting for the book), Stephen is the most loved, because, though unable to speak, he has an incredible ability to touch the hearts and minds of those around him with the power of his personality. While "talking" one day with the letter board, he makes this comment about his power and its source: "Those who are powerful are always those who have come to terms with the helplessness of either aging or disease." Stephen's point—or rather, Peck's—is that all of us are helpless in some ways, but those who are physically or mentally challenged are often more able to come to terms with helplessness, thus releasing their powerful inner forces and deeply affecting lives around them.

As I stated earlier, I believe that none of us is ever in perfect balance in this life. We achieve moments of brilliance, weeks of peak performance, or months of consistency, but none of us is ever fully balanced all the time. So relax!

However, an understanding of how our spiritual framework works in dynamic interaction with our practical planes of existence is key to finding and keeping balance for longer and longer periods. It's possible for any one of us to achieve steady enough equilibrium that a balanced condition is "normal" for us; the out-of-balance moments then become the exception rather than the rule.

I'm confident of this principle because I see it in my own life. There's nothing special about me. I was an average kid from an average family who had average looks and got average grades. A large part of my youth was focused on playing basketball, and then I got cut from the varsity team in my senior year of high school—typical focus, typical setback.

I entered adulthood, then, as an average person with an average background. No great successes or setbacks had influenced me. Things weren't rosy, though. Outbursts of anger were an ugly part of my young-adult life. Oh, I never hit anyone, but I did kick the bathroom door. Splintered wood, broken latches, and bent hinge pins necessitated regular repair jobs in every house we owned. In the language of this chapter, my thoughts were out of control, and my emotions followed. Stress at work or in the family always seemed to heat to the boiling point. Then it occurred to me that I could control my anger by controlling my thoughts. No amount of remorse, praying, or reading self-help books made any difference until I consciously decided to try controlling my thoughts.

It didn't happen overnight. Just ask my sons: they'll be happy to describe their most memorable experience of my "going ballistic," as they call it. Yet in the last eight years not one of our bathroom doors (there are four in this house) has suffered so much as a scratch. It's not that our circumstances have become easier. In fact, the stress during those eight years has been greater than ever; we've faced disappointments, disease, and even death—circumstances that have made the earlier years seem like grade school. So I know that these principles work because they *have* worked, in the most practical ways, for me.

We must be careful, however, to recognize that there are times when our own efforts simply can't overcome the obstacles we face. An airborne virus can invade the body, causing a severe cold that affects our normal physical balance. The fatigue resulting from this imbalance can then affect normal thinking. No amount of positive thinking can kill the virus; it has to be treated medically.

On the other hand, medical science has proven beyond all doubt that positive attitudes, hope, faith, and even prayer greatly affect our immune system (a phenomenon we'll discuss more fully in the next chapter). Sometimes wrong thinking can depress the immune system, thereby allowing a virus to invade and sicken the body. Although the virus is treated and cured, unless the inner cause of a weak immune system is corrected, the cycle will repeat itself over and over. A person with an inner conflict affecting the immune system is subject to far more infections, colds, flus, and even life-threatening diseases than the person with a healthy inner life and a healthy immune system.

Whenever faced with a negative condition, whether physical or mental, we must check on the true source of that illness. Is the cause external, as in the case of Peck's Stephen, or is it internal, as my own outbursts of anger were? To answer that question, we must look at the individual, not at the condition, because many conditions can be both externally and internally caused.

For example, all people suffer at one time or another from mental depression. Doctors tell us that the cause is often related to a chemical imbalance in the brain, and many treat that imbalance with drug therapy in the majority of their depression patients. Witness the great popularity of Prozac and other wonderful drugs.

However, if a person is suffering depression symptoms due to bitterness against a parent, for example, the drug therapy won't treat the root cause. Left untreated, that bitterness will infect some other area of the personality. The depression symptoms may be reduced by the drug, but the person may develop other neurotic or even psychotic symptoms. If the bitterness is treated and relieved, however, the inner cause will dissipate and the person may eventually no longer need the drug therapy.

Conversely, the chemical imbalance causing the depression may have been precipitated by an external source. Perhaps the person worked in a factory for many years breathing fumes that have since been discovered to be toxic. Over time, the chemical reaction of the fumes shifted the normal balance of the body, and the natural chemicals controlling depressed feelings were depleted. No amount of positive thinking or self-examination can relieve this condition, because there's no bitterness or other negative thought pattern causing the body's chemical imbalance. The damage of the fumes must be treated, and the drug therapy may last much longer—perhaps even a lifetime.

The point is that you must give yourself an internal checkup when faced with a negative physical condition. Stop and think honestly, "Is there something out of balance in my inner life that might be causing this illness?" If you conclude that there isn't, then search for external causes. By doing this simple exercise, you will have done the most important thing possible to take control of your own health.

At this point someone might say, "Nice theory, but where did you get your medical degree?" Admittedly, I have none, but I do have years of working with people's spiritual problems and seeing the physical results. Furthermore, every day more and more doctors are joining the growing number of those who look for and help patients find treatment for internal causes of disease symptoms. Recently I was in a conversation with the chief of medicine for the largest hospital in our area. We were talking about the addition of services at the hospital, and I happened to ask how many beds there were. "Three hundred and forty-three," he replied, "and a large percentage of them are occupied by people who would be helped more by a dose of Dr. Peale's treatment than by our treatment."

"What do you mean?" I asked.

"Many of the patients we see have real physical symptoms, but they're brought on by mental and spiritual problems, not physical causes."

Put another way, right thinking is the first step in mental, emotional, and physical health. How, then, can we develop the right kind of thoughts in our mental plane? We begin by drawing those thoughts from the inner spiritual framework and shaping them deliberately.

Again, Saint Paul is a good guide for this journey. He wrote, in Philippians 4:8, "Whatever is true, whatever is noble, whatever is right, whatever is pure, whatever is lovely, whatever is admirable—if anything is excellent or praiseworthy—*think on these things*" (italics mine).

Just think how often our minds are filled with frivolous or even negative material. Researchers tell us that we spend multiple hours watching television every week, passively absorbing what's at best trivial and at worst terrifying. Long ago the communications media found out that we'll pay more to hear what worries us than to hear what cheers us. I'm not sure why this is, but I'm more likely to buy the paper if the dominant headline says, "War Is at Hand," than if it says, "Community Feeds Needy Families." Saint Paul knew we had this tendency. Indeed, it's been a human trait for all of recorded time. That's why he challenged his contemporaries, and us, to think on higher things. But it takes effort to focus our minds in this upward direction. Perhaps *direction* is the key: climbing up always takes more effort than climbing down. At any rate, let's spend a few minutes reflecting on how thoughts can be focused and reshaped by our inner spiritual framework.

The Framework of Faith

Faith is a great source of upward thoughts that can reshape attitudes and behaviors. Once you take the first step of allowing yourself to believe and trust in God, however simply that begins, you find a new source of thinking. An easy place to begin is to reflect on his presence, no matter where you are or what situation faces you. Before faith takes hold, most people leave God in church and don't see his presence in the world around them.

Try this: the next time you have to confront your teenager about curfew, or a co-worker about missed deadlines, or a salesperson about a flawed product, take just fifteen seconds to reflect on God's presence in that situation before opening your mouth. In that short time you'll see the other person's perspective, you'll feel God's power (relieving you of the need for the power of anger), and you'll find better words, inspired by thoughts of God, with which to express yourself. The result will be an improved communication and a quicker satisfactory result. Notice I didn't say an *immediate* satisfactory result. God isn't a magic wand to wave over difficult situations; he's a powerful hand up to the next ledge.

The Framework of Hope

Hope is another excellent source of upward thoughts. I like to think of hope as future-directed; it helps keep your eyes on where you're going, especially when where you are gets hard.

Let me offer another corny cliché—one of the sort that's simple and nutritious and stays with you. When learning to fly, pilots use an instrument called an "artificial horizon." It shows a figure of an airplane in relationship to a line representing the edge between earth and sky. Watching the position of the figure is called "checking the attitude" of the plane to the horizon. See the cliché coming? *Your attitude determines your altitude.*

Hope helps your attitude. Looking ahead to where you're going, like focusing on the horizon, makes what you're going through more bearable.

One technique I use to help my attitude is to collect quotes that stir or inspire me, writing them in my own handwriting in a notebook by category. I then turn often to that notebook and reflect on the great thoughts of others. The very first entry under the heading "Hope" comes from a 1968 campaign speech of Robert Kennedy. I find it all the more moving knowing that he was killed following the speech that articulated this quote: "Some people look at the world the way it is and ask, 'Why?' I prefer to look at the world the way it could be and ask, 'Why not?'"

Focus upward thoughts through the hopeful question "Why not?" and you'll build a mental toughness that can handle anything.

The Framework of Love

Love, for me, is the most difficult of the spiritual factors. When my thoughts are focused on myself and my problems—as they usually are—love demands an outward focus. Being a follower of Jesus Christ, I've found the best technique for gaining upward thoughts through love is to ask, "What would Jesus do?"

The apostle John records that Jesus said, "I am come that they might have life, and have it more abundantly" (John 10:10, KJV). But what did he say about how I should achieve that "abundance"? Well, he said a lot of things about life and relationships and money and the afterlife. However, he gave only two commandments.

The ancient Israelite prophet and leader Moses brought ten commandments from God. But when Jesus was on earth, hundreds of years later, he reduced those commandments to these words: "Love the Lord your God with all your heart and all your soul and with all your strength, and with all your mind, and love your neighbor as yourself" (Mark 12:30–31). The only record of Jesus using the term "*my* commandment" is found in the Gospel of John: "This is my commandment, *that you love each other*" (italics mine).

So the answer to the question, "What would Jesus do?" is simple, but it's not easy: he would show love at all times. The natural follow-up—"How can I show love in this situation?"—leads you directly to higher thoughts.

Pretty lofty concept, huh? Well, let me bring it down to earth with a humble fishing story.

One spring Saturday I promised my three boys, all in grade school at the time, that we would take the boat out for an evening fishing trip if we got all the yardwork done. Well, I let the yard chores take too long and had to race the setting sun as we drove to the lake. In my haste I forgot to unhook the trailer winch before backing the boat into the water. It jerked sideways and began to tip over as I reversed. Hearing the boys' excited shouts, I hit the brakes and hopped out, bumping the electric lock as I slammed the door shut.

So there we were—boat sinking and car locked with keys inside, motor running, and muffler bubbling two inches under water. On the deck of the boat, completely submerged, lay all our jackets, along with the sandwiches; the minnow bucket had tipped over, releasing most of our pleasantly surprised bait into the vast lake. The boys and I released and righted the boat before it sank, but it was about a quarter filled with water.

Stepping back, I paused for just an instant, gearing up to "go ballistic." In that moment the question, "What would Jesus do?" flashed though my mind. "How stupid," I thought. "When did he ever face a mess like this?"

Well, that thought triggered my memory, and I had to admit that Jesus *had* faced a situation that wasn't so very different. Coming upon the disciples one morning, he learned that they had been fishing. They had tried all night, exhausting themselves. Having completely messed up the boat, they were just dragging it ashore. "Wait a minute," Jesus said. "Launch out again and try it on the other side."

Launch out again? Well, all right. I called over the boys (who were already amazed, the expected tantrum having failed to materialize), popped open the back window on our car, and stuck a stick in to hit the offending electric lock. After parking the van, we rounded up three stray minnows, climbed into the boat, and headed for our favorite cove. What happened next sounds so corny it could have been made into a movie script starring Jimmy Stewart, but I swear it's the truth.

Gliding quietly into the cove, we selected one pole and baited one of our precious minnows. We flipped a perfect cast next to a submerged stump. Immediately the line began to fly off the reel as something grabbed the minnow and took off. Something *big*. For twenty minutes we fought a magnificent largemouth bass that dove and jumped and turned us into four screaming maniacs. Finally we netted him, the biggest fish we'd ever caught.

Not a great event in the history of mankind, but it's become a legend in the Fellman chronicles. And it became a lesson to the Fellman father. Letting the inner framework support a higher thought turned a lousy day into an incredible one. The circumstances didn't change; rather, I changed the circumstances by the power of a positive thought.

Key Discoveries

Preparation

As we entered the second part of this book, we began exploring how the inner spiritual framework of a life pyramid supports the outer planes of our mental, emotional, and physical existence. In this chapter we've explored how focusing and raising our thoughts to a higher level, through inner spiritual strength, can change patterns of behavior and even physical health.

We've also discussed the fact that a balanced life isn't something we achieve completely and finally; rather, our spiritual equilibrium is a dynamic condition that we can improve, sustain, and (when we lose our way) recover. Balance doesn't mean complete physical, mental, and emotional perfection. Remember the story of Peck's character Stephen: even though severely "limited," he was powerful because he balanced so well what he had.

Action

1. Take out a sheet of paper and write down two SMART goals for improving the quality of your thinking. One of my best techniques is to read good books. Charlie "Tremendous" Jones, a famous motivational speaker and author, says, "You're the same person today you will be five years from now except for two things: the people you meet and the books you read." Why not formulate one person goal and one book goal? Remember, to be SMART a goal must be

- Specific
- Motivational
- Attainable

- Relevant
- Trackable

2. To provide the time to work on your goals, do a "television check" this week. Watch what you usually watch, and honestly record the time you spend watching it. Then commit yourself, in writing, to spending just *half* of that time in working on your goals from this chapter. Believe me, you can change your life this way. I know, because that's how I wrote this book.

Chapter 8

Using Your Spiritual Framework to Strengthen Your Emotional Being

One benefit of imagining your spiritual framework as a triangular pyramid is that this model clearly indicates strong interrelationships between your mental, emotional, and physical being. I believe that these relationships are linked in a sequence rather than being completely interchangeable. Thoughts generated in your mental life create attitudes. Attitudes govern the use of your emotions. And your mind and emotions, taken together, have a tremendous effect on both your health and the success of any physical endeavor.

Athletes often speak of being "in the zone" when they exhibit peak performance. It's a term used to describe this sequence of attitude to emotion to physical performance. My favorite tennis player is Jimmy Connors, probably because he's a year older than I am and still does incredible things long beyond the age when others have packed it in. After finally giving up the professional "open" circuit, what did Connors do? Something everyone said was impossible: he created a viable commercial tennis circuit for world-class players over thirty-five. Of course, Connors is leading the pack of winners on the new circuit. I imagine that when he loses a step or two in this bracket, he'll launch national tournaments for senior citizens! As Connors illustrates, incredible attitude linked to positive emotion can have amazing physical results.

I've long believed that the centerpiece of this sequence, emotion, is the number-one reason that people succeed or fail in their individual quest to build a balanced and fruitful life. Great attitudes and marvelous physical skills can easily be defeated by runaway emotions.

For years it was my privilege to coach Little League baseball and recreational basketball in our town. I got started in order to spend time with my sons, and by the time the youngest finished with those programs in the eighth grade, eleven years had passed. There were many memorable times, both winning and losing. But the moments I remember best were those when one of the kids caught and benefited from my primary message: "Attitude is everything."

No matter what the game or how good the team, I always insisted that we cheer each other in every possible situation. If the worst batter struck out again, we all yelled, "Great swing; you'll get it next time!" When my smallest basketball player couldn't get the ball high enough to go through the basket in his first year, I insisted that he try at least two or three shots every game. All season long the entire team passed to him and gave him the chance; they caught the spirit and would cheer, "Wow! Almost, Robert, *almost!*" When late in the season a shot finally went in for Robert, our team cleared the bench and had to take a time-out to celebrate. That was two years ago. Most of the players probably don't remember that we went on to lose by two points, but I saw Robert in the grocery store not long ago and he said, "I still remember the first basket, Coach!"

But talent and effort can be wiped out by emotions. One of the best players I ever coached was a boy I'll call Mark. He had talent, dedication, and a real desire to succeed in basketball (because he hoped his hoop skills would gain him a college education).

Mark had everything, including a sometimes-uncontrollable temper. Bigger than the other boys, he was physically intimidating, and when he felt wronged, he often reacted with a body block or a shove. As coach, my view was, "Hey, this isn't the NBA. We're trying to learn this game and have fun." Therefore, I didn't allow an aggressive physical style. Over and over again I pulled Mark from a scrimmage or a game and told him that his temper had to stay under control if he wanted to play on our team. He would listen, but once he was back on the court, he always seemed to believe that his abilities allowed him to break the team rules.

With Mark's leadership and scoring, we won a lot of games that year and ended up number two going into the playoffs. The contest for the town championship was held one cold Saturday morning. The game seesawed back and forth until just before the second half, when the other team made a six-point run. (This was grade-school ball, where most games are won with under forty points, so six points was a big lead.)

Our team was on defense and captured the rebound on a missed shot. Streaking down the court, Mark was wide open for a fast-break shot and yelled for the ball. The pass came a bit short, and as Mark slowed to gather in the ball, an opponent caught up and grabbed his arm to prevent an easy basket. His anger boiling, Mark shoved the other player. Running onto the court, I called for a time-out and took him to our bench to calm him down.

"Mark," I said, "no matter what, we don't play that way. Either you calm down, or I'll bench you. If you lose it again, you're out of the game."

Everybody was quiet, waiting for Mark's response. He said, "Okay, okay, Coach. Let's play ball."

During the second half tension increased as we battled back and regained the lead. With a one-point lead we were back on defense when the other team ran a play that sent a guard driving right into Mark's position under the basket. He saw the collision coming and got himself set to take the bump, hoping to have a foul called on the opposing player.

The referee didn't see it that way. He called a foul on Mark for blocking the path of the offensive player. Our opponent made both free throws and then taunted Mark on the way back up the court. Once again Mark's emotions boiled, and he grabbed the boy and shoved him into the protective mats hanging on the wall behind the basket. The ref whistled a technical, and bedlam ensued.

It seemed as if every parent and kid in that gym was watching me as I went up the court to confront Mark. His anger was still flaring, and he glared at me defiantly. Quietly I said, "You're out of the game, Mark. Go sit on the bench."

"You can't do that, Coach! What about his trash talk? If you take me out now, we'll lose."

"I don't want us to win by beating up the other guys," I replied. "Get back to the bench."

To his credit, he went to the bench without further argument. I substituted another player and we returned to the game. A few plays later we were down by four points with just a minute left to play. A foul sent one of our players to the line, and I called a time-out. As we huddled together to gain composure and talk last-minute strategy, Mark pleaded with me to let him in.

"Please, Coach," he said, "I've learned my lesson; let me go in and we can win. I won't get out of control, I promise."

Across the gym his mother and father were yelling at me to put Mark back in, and I could see that most of his teammates wanted the same thing. Hey, *I* wanted to win too. But Mark meant more to me than that.

"Look," I countered, "we had an understanding, and you broke the rule." Turning to address the whole team, I said, "Although I'd love to win, it's more important that you guys grow up knowing that there's a right way to win and a wrong way to win. Knocking somebody into the wall is the wrong way, and unless Mark learns that today, he might never learn it. The next time somebody could get hurt, and then his basketball career would be over forever."

Mark stayed on the bench, and we lost. The postgame locker-room experience was painful, and accepting the runner-up trophy (knowing we'd had a shot at number one) was bittersweet. Mark's dad read me the riot act for about thirty minutes after the locker room cleared out, and I got a sense of where the boy's anger probably originated. It was the last game Mark played with me; the next year he made the freshman team in high school. The story could have ended there, but it didn't.

Two years later, as a junior, Mark volunteered to referee some of our regular-season games. When one of the players got a little rough, he whistled a foul and said, "Hey, we don't play that way. Don't you listen to anything Coach tells you?"

The knowing grin he flashed at me as he headed up the court was worth all the pain and second-guessing I'd ever done about that championship game—a game when the team lost but Mark won.

Another way to visualize this concept of the sequence from mental attitudes to emotional power to physical results is to think of this particular aspect of life as the energy that flows through the life pyramid. The energy is generated by thoughts, which produce attitudes, which control actions. The energy is itself controlled by emotions: positive emotions open the flow to its maximum physical results, while negative emotions restrict the flow.

Back in the days when I learned to drive, big engines—eight cylinders and lots of horsepower—were popular in cars. A phrase reflecting that interest was commonly used to describe peak performance in any endeavor: "He's running on all eight cylinders." In other words, he's delivering maximum power.

However, those engines had so much potential that you could get a car going on just four cylinders. It didn't run *well*—it rattled and shook, belched smoke, and used up fuel at an alarming rate—but you could get places. *Some* power got through, but not nearly what the engine could deliver if a tune-up put all eight cylinders to work.

That's how emotions work. Like the engine that can get by in a pinch on four cylinders, you can get by with less than full power, but you'll shake, rattle, belch smoke, and use a lot of fuel to get a short distance. An emotional tune-up can put back incredible power—perhaps power you never knew was there.

This chapter will explore balance and strength in your inner spiritual framework as the driving force that shapes and strengthens your outer plane of emotions. However, before we begin to explore that process, there's an important external factor to consider. As with our mental plane, sometimes outside forces—factors in the environment or a chemical imbalance—can override some of the effects of inner balance, requiring treatment. In fact, there's one powerful external force that affects the emotions of our generation almost universally: the pace of life we keep generates a stress that often becomes overwhelming, drowning and defeating any effort to keep emotions under proper control.

I was never much of a history buff, but one of my sons became interested in history during high school and has sustained that curiosity now in college. Seeing his interest and discussing various topics with him, I've been awakened to one incredible difference between our time and that of the 1700s and 1800s, out of which most of our present history was molded. In those days the more successful you were, the more relaxed and slower-paced your life. To be successful was to own land that others worked and to spend the profits on scientific, cultural, or exploratory pursuits. Thomas Jefferson spent more hours during his adult life breeding tomatoes than he did writing the Constitution of the United States or being this country's president.

Today being successful means having a life framed by cellular phones and fax machines. The more successful you are, the faster your modes of travel to get to more destinations per year to do more business so you can travel to even more destinations next year. You have to have a satellite pager so that people can get in touch with you anywhere in the world (and a cellular telephone and a laptop computer so that you can instantly respond).

This is nuts! Let me tell you how I know. I'm writing these words at 5:45 A.M. at a ski resort in Utah, where I'm supposed to be on vacation with my family. I got up, used my cellular phone to call the office back in New York (it opens at 7:30, which is 5:30 in Utah), fired up my laptop to check my e-mail, and then switched programs to work on my goal of writing five pages before everyone else—the seventeen family members and friends I came here to enjoy—gets up at 7:30. Let me repeat, "This is nuts."

So I'm writing this chapter for me as well as for you. Hear me out: I know how the stress of overcommitment can lead to out-of-balance emotions and destroy the peace of days or weeks of your life. But I'm learning how to recognize and handle the stress. This is the first time in five days that I've checked messages at the office, and I *always* get up at 5:00 A.M. because I'm generally asleep by 9:00 the night before. Getting enough sleep is one of the best stress fighters you can use.

Here's the first important point about the negative effects of the pace we keep and the stress it produces: we think we must move faster and faster in order to be successful, and that's simply not true. We're the first generation to have the means to move this quickly, and we conclude that if the means is present, we're obligated to use it more and more efficiently. Wrong. By that logic we should resume the nuclear arms race, and build and use bigger and "better" bombs. We don't need to let the availability of technology control our lives; in fact, we *must* not.

The second (and most important) point about the negative effects of stress is that the pace most of us keep these days defeats our efforts to find meaning and fulfillment. When we began this book together, I expressed my belief that all humans are spiritual creatures and that success and fulfillment are found only when we admit this and begin to actively explore our spirituality and recognize its impact and importance in every area of life. I also expressed my belief that spirituality begins and ends with a very real Supreme Being who knows us, cares about us, and has given guidance on how to maximize this spiritual journey. I call this being God. And God won't move at our accelerated pace. If you want to find God, you must slow down.

There's a great story in the New Testament that addresses this point. When Jesus was an adult and his teaching was gaining popularity, he visited the home of two friends, Mary and Martha. His disciples and other close friends had come with him, and Mary and Martha were hosting lunch. Martha was busy in the kitchen with all the preparations, probably having risen at the crack of dawn to make sure everything was perfect. At that critical point known to every hostess, when everything happens at once and the meal must be served hot, her sister Mary was nowhere to be found.

Martha searched the house and found Mary sitting at Jesus' feet, listening to his teaching. Exasperated, as all of us would be, Martha exclaimed, "Lord, don't you care that my sister has left me to do the work by myself? Tell her to help me!"

"Martha, Martha," Jesus replied. "You are worried and upset about many things, but only one thing is needed. . . . Mary has chosen what is the better part" (Luke 10:38–42).

I'm not sure what Martha did or said next, but I like to think that she sighed, sat down, and spent some time with Jesus. Perhaps after a while he said, "Okay, it's time for lunch. Some of you should go into the kitchen and help Martha and Mary get it ready."

Jesus knew that sometimes we have to let go of the urgent in order to make time for the important. Given the ever-increasing pace that satellite communications and cyberspace information bring to our lives, this is one of the most important lessons needed today. Let me share my experience of learning the power of slowing down in order to handle our speeded-up worlds.

I turned forty in 1994. That birthday wasn't as traumatic for me as for many guys, but the year leading up to it was incredibly pressured. The added pressure of leaving young adulthood behind and slipping into middle age certainly didn't help my psychic or spiritual state, and it played havoc with my emotions. Having watched several older friends go through various levels of trauma during their fortieth year, I had a plan ready well in advance. So when Joy asked, on my thirty-ninth birthday, "What do you want for your birthday next year?" I had an answer ready: "I want a week to myself, no strings attached."

That may not seem like much to you, but it's a lot to ask of a mother of three teenage boys during summer vacation (a time when I usually really help out). But Joy knew I wouldn't ask for something trivial—and besides, she got a new car for her fortieth birthday—so she agreed. Perhaps she wouldn't have if I had told her how I was going to use the time. I had decided to take a week-long solo canoe trip in the Boundary Waters Canoe Area of northern Minnesota.

Starting when I was ten years old, my father often took me to that magical region of lakes, streams, and pine forests. Because of the pressures in his life, we always stayed two, three, or maybe four nights—never a week. I wanted enough time to immerse myself in the adventure. And something told me that it would be a good experience to go by myself. So it came about that in September of 1994 I was headed north on I-35 in a car borrowed from my father, carrying a canoe borrowed from my brother, and packing freeze-dried food, a warm coat, a tiny tent, fishing gear, and my Bible. I was headed into a million acres of wilderness that offered no roads, no phones, and no toilets.

The previous year had been marked by the death of Norman Vincent Peale, my boss, mentor, and friend. As with most men, much of my self-worth was caught up in my job, which was helping to carry on the work Dr. Peale had started at the Peale Center. By that September I wasn't sure what kind of job I was doing. And, like most forty-year-old males, I had figured out that I was never going to come in off the bench for the Chicago Bulls or motorcycle to Alaska.

I had also, in that previous year, sat by a hospital bed with my arm around the shoulders of a good friend as he made the decision to cease life support for his wife of thirty-seven years. The four of us had traveled together just six days earlier, and during that trip a freak fall down some hotel stairs had so damaged her brain that there was no hope left. Never before had I watched someone die, let alone someone so close. By September forty felt very old, and the test-question answers learned in seminary didn't seem to fit anymore.

So, by instinct more than spiritual discipline, I found the power of solitude in the middle of chaos. After three days alone in the north woods, I was soaking wet from the constant rain and cold and hungry because my camping skills were rusty. I had been chased out of my camp by a bear twice. I was about ready to tell God to take a hike.

With no television or telephone to distract me, my Bible got read a lot. Passages I had read over the years began to come to mind easily. Two quotes from the Psalms came to me over and over. The first was, "The heavens declare the glory of God; and the skies proclaim the work of his hands" (Psalm 19:1). The second was, "Be still, and know that I am God" (Psalm 46:10).

The beauty of that wilderness, and the stillness brought on by the absence of modern traffic, entertainment, and office sounds, gradually soaked into me with the rain. On the fourth day I sat on a huge granite boulder overlooking the lake. Wearing my last dry clothes under my rain poncho, I watched as another two inches of precipitation removed any chance of a forest fire in the next decade. As that morning drew to a close, the rain lessened and then stopped, except for the showers that continued for hours as the leaves above me shed their moisture. And because the air was so clear, a double rainbow formed over the lake—a rainbow that I was still enough and *present* enough to really witness. Double rainbows are rare, and double rainbows whose ends are visible are rarer still. This one ended in the lake in front of me.

Although my planned trip schedule called for several miles of paddling that day and a new camping location, I stayed on that rock for hours. The quiet beauty filled my mind and blocked out all my worries about the office, concerns about my teenage sons, and regrets about opportunities precluded by middle age. With my mind full of that beauty, my soul began to rest and life took on a clearer perspective (not new, mind you; just clearer).

The funny thing is that the next year, 1995, should have been one of the most stressful ever. One month after my canoe trip, an unforeseen upheaval hit our organization—a tough blow since we were only beginning to recover from the loss of Dr. Peale. Friends moved away, and my oldest son went off to college, vowing to discover all the adolescent pleasures I had withheld from him at home. Joy began having problems with her blood pressure and experienced chest pains that the doctors couldn't diagnose.

Yet through all this I lived in a much calmer place. When the pressure cranked up the stress meter, I found myself remembering the rock and the rainbow. Even though I didn't get a vacation in 1995, the memory of that place and the power of that solitude created "mini retreats" out of airplane delays and interminable committee meetings. When the pressure grew in the summer, I took Mondays off to keep perspective. Now I've planned my calendar to include solitude—perhaps not a week in the wilderness, but a day here and a weekend there. By reducing the stress on my spiritual framework, I've given it more power to govern my emotions, thereby allowing those emotions to be a better link and creating a better balance between my mental and physical being.

The solitude principle is urgently needed in our lives today, but it's by no means a new concept. The Bible, for example, shows Moses, Jesus, and Saint Paul all undergoing extended periods of aloneness before intense effort. Often the ability to plan, look forward to, and reflect back on a period of solitude can sustain spiritual strength for extended periods—even years.

The spiritual framework of our life pyramid is strengthened by solitude and therefore becomes better able to handle the powerful emotional plane of our outer existence. There are two key needs in respect to emotions: the need to restrict and channel negative emotions (such as anger, jealousy, and envy) and the need to strengthen positive emotions (such as compassion, caring, and joy).

Both sets of emotions are valuable. One of the best examples of valuable negative emotions I've seen is the organization MADD (Mothers Against Drunk Driving). Out of the grief and anger over the drunk-driving deaths of their teenagers, a group of mothers created an organization that has saved countless lives, young and old. Instead of allowing grief to freeze their hearts, they used it to stir the hearts of others. Instead of allowing anger to shrivel their spirits, they used it to pass laws, encourage alternatives, and promote awareness in Congress, the media, schools, and communities nationwide.

Flip the coin and you have positive emotions changing the face of entire nations—in India through the compassion and caring of Gandhi and in South Africa through the forgiveness and cooperation of Nelson Mandela. Let's look specifically, then, at how your inner spiritual framework can be used both to channel negative emotions and to strengthen positive ones.

The Framework of Faith

Exercising belief and trust in God when dealing with emotions is the first step toward controlling and strengthening them. Emotions are a tremendous source of energy, but they—like nuclear energy—can be a power for either destruction or good. Putting God into the picture along with our emotions causes a tremendous creative reaction to take place. No longer are we totally responsible for emotional outcomes. In one of the mightiest paradoxes of spirituality, when we're weakest, God's strength is most evident.

Sometimes our emotions have to break us down in order for us to find new strength. Every recovered alcoholic knows the power of the Twelve Steps, one of which is to admit weakness and call out to God (however the person knows him) for help. Millions of hurting people have been helped by the poem "Footprints," by Margaret Fishback Powers. Perhaps you've read it. It tells the story of a person looking back on the footprints he left in the sand as he moved through life—footprints that for much of life's journey were matched by a second set of prints belonging to God. Over some of the stretches, though—the hardest patches of life—only a single set of footprints marked the sand. The person puzzles over this, wondering why God had abandoned him in life's toughest moments. God replies gently, "My child, those were the times I carried you." Jesus himself articulated this principle when he said to Saint Paul, "My grace is sufficient for you, for my power is made perfect in weakness" (2 Cor. 12:9).

Many people go through life with damaged emotions and never know this principle of power in weakness. Difficult experiences in childhood often warp a young person's emotions and lead to a crippled adult. A new therapy called "healing of memories" has recently been developed to help people deal with childhood trauma that damaged emotions and limited the person as an adult. However, this therapy, without a spiritual base, is in my opinion very dangerous. Without a belief and trust in God, none of us is strong enough to handle all the hits we take in life. What good does it do to break down the door to a locked cellar if what you find is so slimy, dank, and putrid that you're powerless to clean it up by yourself? It seems to me that more damage is done with that approach than by keeping the door closed. However, if you take God by the hand and let him kick down the door and go in with a mop and a bucket, then real cleaning can take place.

The entire house of your life is refreshed and restored, revealing incredible possibilities. The first (and primary) result of allowing faith to handle emotions is the release of a powerful hope.

The Framework of Hope

Once the grip of negative emotions is broken through faith, the power of positive emotions can be released through hope. By generating the expectation for success, you and I can achieve incredible results in our daily lives and in our lifetime dreams. One of the greatest examples of this process is Dr. Henry Viscardi.

The son of Italian immigrants in the United States, Henry "Hank" Viscardi was born in 1912 with only stumps for legs. He stands only three feet eight inches tall without support, but thousands have come to know him as a giant of a man.

When he was still small, the taunts and stares of people got to be too much one day, and he cried out to his mother, "Why me?"

"When it was time for another crippled boy to be born," she replied, "the Lord and his councils held a meeting to decide where he should be sent, and the Lord said, 'I think the Viscardis would be a good family to take care of him.'"

Hank held on to that answer and used his dry wit and sharp mind to breeze though grade school and high school in New York City. Fitted with pads for his stumps, he worked his way through Fordham University sweeping floors and waiting tables. But using the stumps of his legs as feet gradually incapacitated the stumps; by college graduation he faced life in a wheelchair. One orthopedic doctor held out the slimmest hope: perhaps artificial limbs could be made. Hank took that hope to heart, fanned it into a flame, and began to visit artificial limb makers. One after another, they turned him down. He hadn't *lost* his legs, they said;

he'd never had any, making the task impossible. Finally one German limb maker saw the hope in Hank's eyes and gave it a try.

Months later, at twenty-seven years old, Hank stood up straight for the first time. He looked in the mirror at all five feet eight inches of his profile and was overwhelmed. When he asked the doctor what he owed, the doctor replied, "There's no bill now. But someday, if you'll make the difference for one other individual—the difference between a life dependent on charity and one rich with dignity and self-sufficiency—our account will be squared."

Hank did much more than that. He served in World War II as a Red Cross officer helping amputees. Returning home, he was shocked at how these veterans who had given so much were treated. No jobs were available to them; often they couldn't even get interviews. He began to speak to business leaders about the injustice, urging them to help his cause. Soon several of them founded Just One Break (JOB) and asked Henry to run the program. He did so with great success, but the experience just emphasized for him all that needed to be done. In 1952 he started an organization called Abilities, Inc., to prove that, given a chance, the physically handicapped can work effectively in industry.

Over the years the organization has grown; it's now known as the National Center for Disability Services. Through it Hank pioneered efforts in the education and rehabilitation of people with disabilities, especially children. Today, in his eighties, Hank serves as president emeritus of the center, the heart of which is the Henry Viscardi School. That school's 220 students, ranging from kindergartners through high schoolers, are all severely physically challenged. Hank created the tuition-free school to provide a place where young people can learn and grow and build the brighter future his doctor charged him with so long ago.

Hank Viscardi once told a luncheon group I was part of that his faith-filled hope in God provided the vital ingredient to discovering how his life could be made full. "Without that hope," he said, "my life would have been empty and meaningless. I can't help but believe that the Lord had a plan for my life that made me the way I was and let me become who I am."

The Framework of Love

The third piece of our inner spiritual framework that channels and strengthens our emotions is love. It comes last because it follows a belief and trust in God, which leads to expectation for success. In fact, many would say that love is itself an emotion. To me, though, love is much more than *an* emotion. It's emotion in motion, to again borrow Walter Trobisch's phrase. Love is the conduit through which positive emotional energy, channeled and strengthened by faith and hope, flows out to others without regard for the return to ourselves.

Love lets us see another starving child on another news report and respond as if it were the first starving child we had ever seen. Love eliminates the weariness of dealing one more time with a cranky in-law, difficult boss, or wayward teenager. Faith and hope are often directed inwardly, helping the individual become stronger. Love, which is outward-directed, puts that strength to work. Love can be tough and channel anger so that it becomes a positive, corrective force, as when we confront an unjust situation or intervene in the life of a person trapped in substance abuse. Love can be as gentle as a cooling rain on a summer afternoon, giving joy to an aged parent or bonding two people with so many tiny, gentle threads that a marriage lasts a half-century or more. But love of any kind controls emotions and forces them to flow for the good of another, no matter the hurt or difficulty to the one giving the love.

Earlier in this chapter I mentioned sitting with a good friend as his wife died. Those moments offered one of the greatest lessons in love I've ever learned. Once the doctors had explained the medical facts, my friend had to decide for his wife what she would want. Having been married to her a long time, he knew she wouldn't want machines keeping her alive if there were no hope of recovery, so he chose to remove the machines.

If I had been in his place, I would have signed the papers, left the room, and gone somewhere to cry. But my friend wanted to stay. His children couldn't bear it; hugging first their mother and then their father, they left the room. The nurse assisted the doctor with various preparations and then gently touched my friend on the shoulder. "I'm so sorry," she said, and she left the room. Finally the doctor removed the last tubes and wires and said, "I'll be outside if you need me." He too left the room.

I was shocked by the speed and finality of the whole process and uncomfortable at being left without the medical team. I wanted to be anywhere but there. But when my friend looked up and said, "You'll stay, won't you, Eric?"

"Sure," I croaked, wanting to be anywhere else.

Together we watched her chest rise and fall more and more slowly. At one point he took her hand and lay his forehead on it at the side of the bed. I watched on alone. First the breathing stopped; then the beating of her heart was still. After a few minutes I said, "She's gone now."

With a deep sigh he lifted his head, kissed her, and said, "Good-bye, my darling."

Turning to me, he said, "Thanks for staying. You see, I *had* to stay, because thirty-seven years ago we promised to stick by each other 'until death us do part,' and I wasn't going to leave until she did. But I wouldn't have made it alone."

There was no joy or feeling of success that day—only the overwhelming peace that came from being there when emotion was framed by Hope and Faith, channeled through Love, and used to begin the healing process that all of us need at sometime in our lives.

Key Discoveries

Preparation

In this chapter we've explored emotion, the second of the three external planes of our lives. Set into the framework of the life pyramid, the shape is illustrated in the figure below.

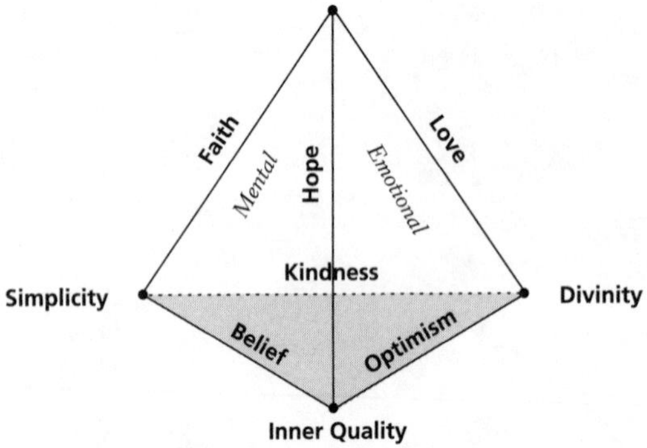

This chapter on emotion falls where it does—in the middle of our discussion of how the inner spiritual framework holds together, balances, and shapes the external planes—because emotions are a powerful force in themselves. Controlling and channeling negative and positive emotions so that they become energy that adds to life instead of subtracting from it requires a strong framework. Emotions are the link between our mental and physical lives. Good attitudes and good physical conditioning can be defeated by negative emotions.

In order to hold the emotional plane in balance, we need to strengthen the spiritual framework by managing the stress that weakens it. Once that stress is reduced or controlled—perhaps with the help of solitude—Faith, Hope, and Love combine to shape and channel the power of emotions.

Action

Here are three steps you can take to build your inner strength and manage your emotions instead of being managed by them:

1. Do an emotional self-evaluation. Ask yourself the following questions:

Have my emotions overheated three or more times in the last week?

Have I felt numb emotionally for more than a few hours in the last week?

Have I experienced joy three or more times in the last week?

Can I remember at least two times in the last month when negative emotions, under control, produced positive results?

The last time I really competed for something, did emotion help me?

The most balanced answers are no, no, yes, yes, yes. If you have the opposite answer to two or more questions, stress may be letting emotions run outside the control of your inner spiritual framework.

2. Now administer a stress self-evaluation—either informally (by listing recent stressors in your life and weighing their impact) or formally. Even a simple stress evaluation that gives points for life events such as moving, death of a friend, marriage, divorce, and so on can be very helpful. One tool I've found very helpful is the "Social Adjustment Rating Scale" by Rahe and Holmes. It takes into account major events like a new job or death in the family and adds up your "Life Change Units." When you exceed a certain number of points on such a test, your stress level is too high.

3. Take the results of the first two exercises and develop a plan to add solitude to your life in order to strengthen your inner spiritual

framework. You may not choose to go into the wilderness for forty days, as Jesus did (or even seven days, as I did), but try this simple test. Find a way to be alone in a room for three hours with no work and no distractions—no television, no reading material, no phone calls, no writing, no work. If you can be alone in that room and enjoy the company, you have a healthy leg up on using solitude. If you can't, you need to work on enjoying your own company and listening to the voice of God within you. Remember, he won't move as fast as we do, and he won't shout over the noise we put into our lives.

Chapter 9

Using Your Spiritual Framework to Strengthen Your Physical Being

As we move to considering the third and final external plane of our lives—the physical—the life pyramid takes on its final shape. The inner spiritual framework has now been complemented by the three planes of mental, emotional, and physical being.

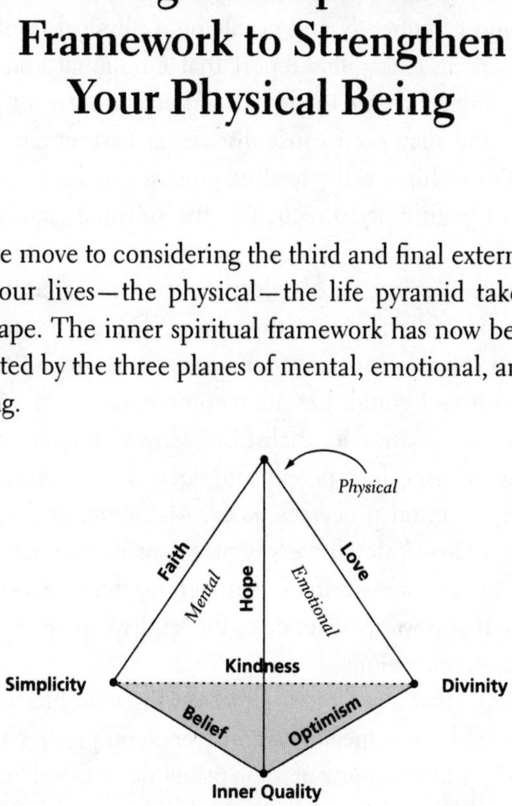

We've discussed how these three planes are linked together in a sequence, with the central emotional plane having great influence over mental and physical well-being. The best way to control emotions is to remove stress from the spiritual framework and use the elements of faith, hope, and love to channel emotional energy so that it positively affects our mental and physical being.

These principles and the truths they represent are most dramatically seen in the physical realm. The interaction between our spiritual framework and our mental and emotional planes surfaces most frequently and visibly on a physical level. That's why doctors and hospitals report that emotional and mental problems often increase the length of hospital stays for physical problems and may even cause disease; at best, emotional and mental distress hinders the healing process. Medical professionals are just beginning to recognize the spiritual factors in this process.

It's not my purpose here to document the research, the medical and scientific evidence of this process. Dozens of good books in the past several years have done a better, more authoritative job at that than I could. Let me recommend two. *Healing and the Mind,* by television journalist Bill Moyers, documents (with research and cases) how people and doctors have affected healing though mental processes. *Love, Medicine, and Miracles,* by physician and Yale University professor Bernie Siegel, documents the deeper spiritual connection that drives mental processes. If you want evidence of the truths I share here, these two books are marvelous.

Dr. Siegel had a profound effect on my own life when Dr. Peale invited him to speak at a conference on positive thinking in 1985. My understanding of these principles was just beginning to grow, and I regret to say I was doubtful that a Jewish doctor from Yale University could have much of value to say to a largely Christian audience of positive thinkers. I could hardly believe it when he announced the title of his speech as "Love, Medicine, and Miracles" (this was just prior to the book's publication). For the next hour I was spellbound as he told how he had changed as a doctor and a person by applying the principles of spiritual faith to medical practice. Two important things he said in that speech have been borne out by countless articles in medical and popular journals I've read since that time. These principles form the basis of truth about the interconnection of spiritual being and physical being:

1. If you want to learn how to live, find someone who could be dead tomorrow and decides not to be and learn from that person.
2. All improvement requires change, yet most of us would rather be ruined than change. Change takes courage.

The first principle deals with the biggest physical fear most of us have: the fear of dying. Since all of us die (though Siegel says he's met a few surgeons who think they're exceptions), death, by definition, can't be a failure. Therefore, the only failure is not living. When you find a person who's physically surviving against great odds, you find a very successful person; study him or her.

One of Siegel's patients, a woman named Marie, gave him a simple yet very important lesson when she said, "I have stones in my gallbladder, cancer in my breast, and arthritis in my knees, but I'm not my body. I'm a spirit, and my spirit lives and is free."

Only a person with a strong and balanced spiritual framework can live with that passion. Only with such a framework is the mental life strong enough to overcome physical limitations. Only then does the emotional life create such positive energy that physical challenges become secondary.

When he was a young doctor, Siegel (like most doctors) was taught not to get involved with his patients beyond their diseases. "Your judgment will be impaired," his teachers threatened. "You'll exhaust yourself emotionally," they warned. But early in his career Siegel began to ask his cancer patients what they needed most from him. Over and over the replies went something like: "You look me over and tell me to come back in three months, but you don't tell me how to live through those next three months."

As he began to search out ways to help them live, Siegel received from a patient a quote, printed on a card, that shaped his approach toward future practice: "When you were born, you cried and the world rejoiced. Live your life in such a way that, when you die, you rejoice and the world cries."

Inspired by that saying, Siegel began teaching patients how to live so that they could rejoice when life was over. He took as a motto this quote: "If you're alive this moment, your mission in life isn't over. Live it out!" Over and over he was astounded by the results. Patients who had been thought to be terminal walked out of the hospital and lived productive days, months, and even years. But through it all Siegel found that the most crucial factor in being able to live well was the ability to change.

Over and over he would advise patients to forgive anyone against whom they harbored long-standing anger. He'd challenge them with words such as these: "If you knew that the car you were going to ride home in was going be hit by a cement truck and you'd die today, who would you call and what would you say? Here, take my phone, call that person, and say it!"

"I knew the patients who would improve," he recalls, "by the ones who took up my offer."

In this process Siegel learned a great lesson about pain: it's the motivating force behind change. "When you hurt enough," he says, "you'll change or die."

Many of us have seen evidence of this related to addictions, whether in our own lives or the lives of close family and friends.

When people hurt enough inside—or realize how badly they've hurt those they love—they're driven to change.

My father-in-law was wounded in World War II and learned to smoke in order to take his mind off the pain, because he was afraid of addiction to morphine. What he got instead was addiction to tobacco. For forty years that addiction persisted, until one day his doctor told him that another month of cigarettes would kill him. Looking at his kids and grandkids, he decided that the pain of leaving them prematurely was reason enough for him to kick the habit almost overnight.

The power of mind and emotions in the physical realm is often used to promote peak performance. Athletes use mental focus and emotional pitch to earn trophies and set records. However, because most of us aren't in this category, the best use of this principle is to be not *the* best but *your* best. A forty-something guy with twenty extra pounds and flat arches like me may never win even the local basketball shootout, but I can use mental focus and emotional pitch to make the best of what I have; if I push aside the second dessert and take on aerobic exercise twenty minutes a day, three times a week, I can increase my physical potential beyond what it used to be.

Applying the strength of the inner spiritual qualities of faith, hope, and love to our physical being can produce tremendous—sometimes even astounding—personal results.

The Framework of Faith

A couple of years ago one of the Peale Center board members introduced me to his daughter's fiancé. Keiran Delamere told me a story of faith overcoming physical difficulty that wasn't just astounding, it was amazing.

When he was fifteen, Keiran went to the beach with his younger brother and some friends on a sunny morning. Like most big brothers, he couldn't help himself when it came to the occasional harassment of his younger sibling. As Keiran ran along the beach that morning, he veered right through the sandcastle being built by his brother and friends and dashed down to the water to dive in. He took what he thought was a shallow dive into the waves, but he hit the bottom straight on with enough force to break his neck, experiencing instant paralysis.

"There I was, face down in the water, and I couldn't even turn my head to breathe," Keiran recalls. "Somehow I knew I wasn't going to survive, so I prayed, 'God, forgive me for any bad things I've done and please take me into heaven.' Then I simply believed I would die."

As water flowed into Keiran's lungs and darkness swept him into unconsciousness, his brother realized something was very wrong. Yelling to his friends to help, he and the other boys dragged Keiran to the edge of the surf so that his face was just out of the water. One boy squeezed his stomach, expelling enough water to allow Keiran to cough and get shallow breaths. In a whisper he told his brother to run for help.

Keiran doesn't remember much of the rest of that day, but the rush to the hospital brought only worse news. Doctors told his family that he had broken the fifth cervical vertebra and that the extent of his paralysis could be severe. More tests were done in subsequent hours, and after another day the doctors told Keiran's father that he would be a quadriplegic; there simply was no hope of a more positive prognosis.

"My father immediately ordered that no one tell me this news," Keiran recalls. "He told me only that I was hurt but would get better. He wanted me to believe in the possibilities, and he wanted all of our friends to begin praying to see what the power of faith could do."

Keiran had a strong spiritual background, even at fifteen. He and his family were dedicated attenders of church and great believers in prayer. But after several days with no sensation anywhere except his head, Keiran needed something to believe in.

"I remember there was a little red light above my head," he recalls. "I didn't know it then, but it was to call the nurses' station. Being unable to move, I couldn't press the button to turn on the light, of course. Hour after hour I stared at that light, and finally I prayed, 'Lord, if I'm going to walk again, please flash that light.' Just at that moment, it blinked once. From then on I knew I was going to walk. It took a long time to convince the doctors, however."

For three and a half months, Keiran waged a battle against paralysis, armed only with the weapons of prayer and physical therapy. He asked that his arms and legs be moved to avoid atrophy. A tingling sensation gradually returned to his upper body, and after three months he could, as he said, "flap my wings a little bit." Still no feeling returned to his legs or hands, however. During this time, the thousands of people who had heard about his condition through his church were supporting Keiran. Around the world, and probably around the clock, people were praying for him. Finally there were some "trace" muscle movements, but the doctors labeled them involuntary spasms.

After three and a half months, with nothing more positive to point to than the so-called involuntary spasms, the doctors, nurses, and physical therapists held a conference with Keiran and his parents around his bed. For about twenty minutes they went through all the medical evidence. They asserted their reluctant but unanimous opinion that the spasms were all Keiran would ever experience, and they urged the family to begin to accept reality. A moment of silence followed this logical plea, and then his mother quietly replied, "We're deeply grateful for all you've done, and we know you're being realistic and scientific. But you must understand that we believe in a powerful God. We believe he can let Keiran walk again."

Frustrated, the medical professionals filed out of the room. Suddenly Keiran began to feel tingling in his toes, and then more tingling, and he concentrated as hard as he could on moving them. "From this time there's one deeply clear memory I have. Every morning, when I would wake up, there was my father, sitting by my bed, holding my unfeeling hand and praying quietly that I would walk again. The power of that praying and his faith seemed to energize me."

In fact, Keiran was getting better. Soon he could move his toes and even raise his foot a fraction of an inch for just a second or two. But he was so excited that he awakened early each morning and worked so hard to increase this movement that by the time the doctors came by on their rounds he was exhausted and couldn't move! His inability to show them the movement that he claimed to be capable of simply gave the doctors more evidence that the paralysis was permanent.

"Finally I got smart and forced myself to do nothing one morning until the doctors appeared. 'Let me show you how I can move my foot,' I pleaded."

"You say that every morning, Keiran. This can't be good for you. If we do a test right now and you don't pass, will you please start to accept your paralysis?"

"Okay," Keiran replied, confident that he'd never have to make good on his word.

"Fine," said the doctor. "I want you to move your toes, but not until I tell you to and exactly when I tell you to. I'll count to three. When I hit three, you move your toes. If, as I suspect, they don't move, we're going to put this nonsense behind us. Okay: one, two, three." Keiran moved his toes; then he moved his foot. Then he concentrated and did the hardest physical thing he'd ever done in his life: he lifted his foot off the bed. Needless to say, the doctor and all his colleagues were amazed. From that point on aggressive therapy was ordered, and within four weeks, with the aid of a walker, Keiran took his first steps.

However, his battles with the doctors weren't over. Now that his mobility was improving so well, they were concerned about his weakened neck. They recommended surgery to fuse the vertebrae and give him a permanent "stiff neck." Keiran and his parents refused. The doctors said that they wouldn't be responsible for him without that surgery—the risk was simply too great—so Keiran's parents took him home. Within six months he was walking without braces. Today he has a slight limp, but otherwise he has full mobility. He's an insurance salesman with a mission—a mission to help other accident victims find the faith to make the most of hopeless situations.

"It was prayer that increased my faith," Keiran says. "It was prayer that built my faith and helped me believe that anything was possible. And it was that belief that overcame the physical 'reality' of my injuries."

The Framework of Hope

Hope is also a powerful tool in maximizing our physical potential. Indeed, hope is the most important ingredient in healing. Doctors like Bernie Siegel have documented over and over that when two patients have similar diseases and prognoses—one patient with hope and one with no hope—the hopeful patient recovers faster. If the patient without hope recovers at all, it's much more slowly.

Remember, we're talking here about making the most of what we have, not always getting the dramatic results Keiran Delamere achieved. Dr. Siegel tells of many cancer patients who should have died in the hospital but found reason to hope—reason enough to go home to weeks, months, even years of fulfilling life. Although all of us die eventually, through spiritual focus applied to our physical being we can exercise greater control than we ever thought possible over the length and quality of life before death.

Through the nine years I worked closely with Dr. Peale, I listened to him tell many stories about the power of hope. My favorite was of a little African-American girl named Wilma, born to poor parents in rural Tennessee. At a young age she suffered from scarlet fever and was left with a crippled left leg. But Wilma's parents, especially her mother, were filled with hope and passed it along to Wilma. Rather than let her sit in self-pity, her mother set tasks that challenged the limits of Wilma's ability and taught her to stretch herself.

The backdoor to their modest house had a football-sized rock to hold it either open or closed. Wilma's mother challenged her one day to move that rock with her crippled leg. "But I can't, Mother!" exclaimed Wilma.

"You'll never know unless you try," came the reply. "Besides, if you *do* move that rock, someday you'll walk stronger and straighter."

There was nothing Wilma wanted more than to walk like normal children, so she tried to move the rock. At first it wouldn't budge. Then came the day when it moved an inch, and then a foot, and finally she was shoving it all around the back porch. The power of hope so caught hold inside Wilma that even her mother couldn't believe her next goal: "I'm going to be the fastest woman runner in the world," said Wilma.

She could hardly walk straight when she decided to run. But Wilma always remembered how that rock hadn't moved at all until she kept at it and at it. So she began a loping gait up and down her driveway. Then she went down the road a bit. Finally, as a freshman in high school, she entered a race. She came in last. Now Wilma's mother was a devout Christian and had seen the wonder of hope in her daughter's eyes. So when Wilma came home that evening after her first race, her mother called her into the bedroom. Sitting open on her lap was a Bible. She said, "Wilma, I want you to listen to what Saint Paul had to say about running," and she quoted Hebrews 12:1: "Let us throw off everything that hinders . . . run with the perseverance the race marked out for us." Then she turned to Philippians 3:13–14: "Forgetting what is behind and straining toward what is ahead, I press on toward the goal . . ."

She needn't have worried. Wilma had no thought of quitting. She ran the next race. And came in last. She ran the race after that. And came in last. She ran the fourth race. And came in second to last. Within a year she'd won her first race, and after that race she rarely did anything but win. She kept running and running until at last Wilma Rudolf went to the 1960 Olympics in Rome as a runner for the United States of America.

At the time, the women's world record holder in shorter distances was one person, Yetta Hynie of Germany. No one believed that anyone, let alone Wilma, had a chance against Yetta in 1960. However, people forgot to inform Wilma that she didn't have a chance. The first race was the 100-meter sprint, and Wilma won her qualifying heats and then beat Yetta in the final to take the gold medal. Next came the 200-meter; almost like clockwork, the results were the same. The crippled girl from a poor community in Tennessee had two Olympic gold medals in two days. Yet the story didn't end there. The next day came the women's 400-meter relay. Wilma ran last, in the anchor position.

The first three runners did well for the American team, and the handoffs—the critical element in any relay—were flawless. When the third runner rounded the last turn and approached Wilma to pass the baton for the final leg, the American team was leading, with the German team just a few steps behind. Once again Wilma was pitted against Yetta Hynie, but this time everything was in Wilma's favor. Then suddenly that all changed. In her excitement, Wilma dropped the baton. She was at full speed, and it went flying backward. Stopping to retrieve it, Wilma saw Yetta go past her in a blur. All hope for the gold was lost. Well, except in the mind of Wilma Rudolf.

From somewhere deep inside her, Wilma found an incredible burst of speed that came in an instant and was sustained through the entire 100-meter leg of her run. That burst found her gaining on Yetta from the moment Wilma recovered the baton. As the seconds flew by, the crowd watched—first in stunned silence, then in a crescendoing roar, as Wilma broke the finish tape a fraction ahead of Yetta. The impossible had been achieved for the third time!

Why do I tell you the story of Wilma Rudolf? I guess to make the same point, in as forceful a way as I can, that Dr. Siegel made in that speech in 1985: "There's no false hope. All hope is real." By everyone's account, Wilma should have walked with a pronounced limp and simply been happy to be alive. But her hope of winning races was a real thing. It powered her to achievements far beyond expectations. Are you ever tempted to say, "I'm weak; my brother has all the brains in the family; my sister has all the good looks"? How about "I haven't got the contacts I need for success; I never finished my education; I've never done very well; I'm not physically well"? When thoughts of that nature come to you, do me a favor: remember Wilma Rudolf.

Hope raises the level of accomplishment, the level of possibility. Hope can heal. Hope can drive out disease. Hope can overcome any difficulty. It's a real force, and one more powerful than cellular structure, bank accounts, or report cards.

The Framework of Love

Love is another powerful force that can bring about physical results far beyond what we imagine. Like the effects of hope and faith, the effects of love have been scientifically measured recently. Dr. Siegel tells of a group of students who were shown a film of Mother Teresa ministering to the poor in India and asked to record their responses. According to those responses, the students fell into two groups: some were bored or disgusted with the terrible conditions portrayed and wanted to forget the experience as soon as possible; others were deeply moved by the compassion and love they saw displayed by the nun.

Both groups were tested, before and after viewing the film, for the volume of immune globulin present in their blood. Immune globulin is a chemical that the body produces, when prompted by the brain, as its first line of defense against disease. The greater the volume of immune globulin in our blood, the better chance we have to ward off infection from disease or injury.

In both groups—the students who liked the film and those who didn't—immune globulin had increased after the film was shown. In other words, the impact of divine love was present whether the students wanted it or not! The positive effects of love happened to even the most jaded and insensitive. Love was an irresistible force, improving and shaping the students through the simple vehicle of a film about love in action.

Indeed, we can't survive without love. Dozens of studies done with newborn babies have proved that fact. You can feed, clothe, change, and keep babies warm in a nursery, but unless babies are held and loved, they die. We can't survive without love and its physical expression, touch. On the other hand, the power of love to touch and change people is incalculable.

My job takes me into a lot of airplanes during the course of a year. Every once in a while, after I've traveled some magic number of miles, the airline sends me a coupon allowing me to fly first class on my next trip. This is such a treat that I always look forward to those trips—lots of leg room, a wider seat, better meals, and a hot towel to wipe my face with when we arrive at our destination. But since I usually travel economy class, I also feel a bit guilty sitting there in comfort as all the other passengers file past and try to squeeze in three across while tucking their knees in under their chins.

Needless to say, traveling first class puts me in a good mood. So it hits me pretty hard when someone gets into the first-class cabin and starts complaining. Not long ago this was the case with a sharply dressed younger man who was arguing loudly with the ticket agent as he came down the ramp; we could hear him even before he got on the plane. It seems something had gone wrong with his schedule, and he was insistent that she call ahead to Cincinnati, where we were going, to hold the plane he wanted to catch on connection. She could do nothing of the sort, of course, and he was giving her an earful of theological terms (though used in a very unholy manner).

As luck would have it, his seat was across the aisle and one ahead of mine, so I was subjected to his continuing complaints about the limited space in the overhead compartment, the negligible softness of the pillow, the glare of the sun off the wings, and the sound of the engines. After half an hour of this, my enjoyment of first-class seating was almost wiped out by his grumpy demeanor. I was about to say something to try to shame him into shutting up when a startling thought ran through my mind.

What if I simply loved him instead? Now don't get me wrong; I'm not someone who can go up to a stranger and give him or her a hug. But I decided to try a less obvious loving technique that Dr. Peale had taught me—one I'd used from time to time.

This technique involves simply sending out silent, loving thoughts directed at the person you wish to love. I started by first sending this thought across: "I hope you can relax from whatever's bothering you and enjoy this flight." I followed that with, "Isn't the seat nice and comfortable? Don't the clouds look fantastic?" Next came, "Hey, pal, isn't this food great? It's a whole lot better than the fast food or hot pretzels we would've had in the airport if the flight had been canceled."

Within a few minutes my grumpy fellow traveler had quieted down, and he even grunted his thanks when the attendant brought his meal. I kept the thoughts flowing for at least an hour for good measure. The results were amazing: as the guy got up to leave, he glanced at me—a total stranger whom he'd never noticed before—and flashed me a small smile. Love is *real.* It works wonders. Love can change things.

This kind of love is strong; it's not the mushy feeling of dizziness that some people associate with love. Real love in the real world faces problems and crises and hits them head on, cutting them down to size and reducing their impact on the life of the one doing the loving (and on those around him or her). Here's Saint Paul's famous definition again (from 1 Cor. 13:4–7, 13), this time in a different translation (LB). It's worth rereading:

> *Love is patient and kind, never jealous or envious, never boastful or proud, never haughty or selfish or rude. Love does not demand its own way. It is not irritable or touchy. It does not hold grudges and will hardly even notice when others do it wrong. It is never glad about injustice, but rejoices whenever truth wins out.*

If you love someone, you will be loyal to him no matter what the cost. You will always believe in him, always expect the best of him, and always stand your ground in defending him. . . . There are three things that always remain—faith, hope and love—and the greatest of these is love.

That kind of love makes a difference in every life it touches—especially the life of the one doing the loving.

Key Discoveries

Preparation

In this chapter we've examined how our physical lives are supported and enhanced by our spiritual framework, and we've looked at the power of Faith, Hope, and Love to overcome physical setbacks and maximize physical potential. The key discovery should be that much more is possible, both in healing and in the changing of physical circumstances, than most of us imagine if we fail to consider the spiritual factors. In order to maximize our own potential we must force ourselves to learn that the spiritual factors are more important than any medical, psychological, or scientific evidence or experience. In short, miracles do happen when we open ourselves to the possibilities. (I define a miracle as something beyond what would be expected through "natural" means or expectations.)

Before we close this chapter, I want to summarize the key thoughts touched on in Part 2. At the outset we took the framework of the life pyramid and filled in the planes of our external being—mental, emotional, and physical. I tried to show how the spiritual framework of Faith, Hope, and Love supplies the strength behind the external elements and attempted to give practical advice for using the entire spiritual framework to shape and maximize the mental, emotional, and physical planes of our existence. So now our symbolic diagram of the life pyramid, on the next page, is complete.

It's important to remind ourselves that the life pyramid is a living symbol. Our pyramid begins with the foundations of Belief, Optimism, and Kindness, upon which can be built the framework of Faith, Hope, and Love. Then, like trees in a forest that can be shaped into a building, these pieces must be aligned with a spiritual reference point to form a balanced triangular pyamid. Once properly aligned, the framework can support a balanced exterior life represented by the planes of mental and physical existence, which are linked by emotions.

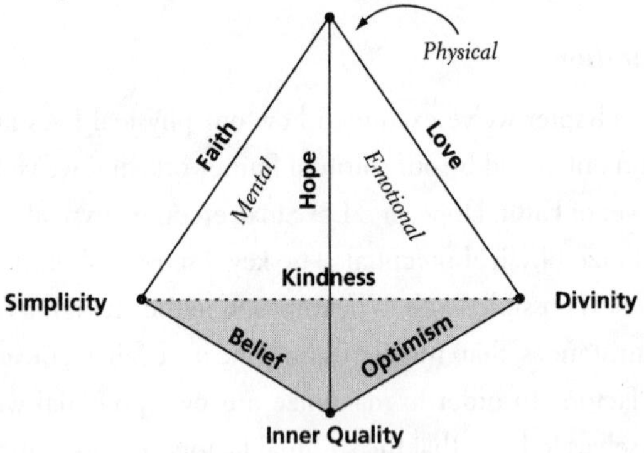

Action

1. Take Dr. Siegel's advice: if you want to learn how to live, get to know someone who has a "terminal" illness and has decided to fight it with everything he or she has. Those people have learned how to live and can teach you much.
2. Make a list of the calls you would make if you knew that today was your last day on earth. Then take the next step: actually make those calls. The peace and emotional energy you release will discharge great power into your life.
3. Like Wilma Rudolf, find something very difficult you've thought of attempting in your life and give it a try; get the process underway. Maybe it's finishing college as an adult or repairing a marriage that looks like a disaster. Whatever the task is, it can't be harder than running your way into the Olympics on a crippled leg, so give it a try.

This process of growing and building takes a lifetime. It's a journey, not a destination. In Part 3 we'll look at tools that can help the process at every stage.

PART THREE

Tools for Finding and Building Your Spiritual Potential

Our description of the life pyramid is almost complete. Although, like any symbol, it can't tell *everything* about our lives, I hope you'll find the pyramid useful as you take the journey toward discovering and energizing your spiritual potential. However, the question Dr. Siegel used to get from his patients haunts me too: How should we live our lives? I assume that if you've read this far, you've found my description of a method of looking at life helpful. Yet like Dr. Siegel sending his patients home, I don't feel that I've given you enough to get you through until the next check-up. The great theologian Francis Schaeffer wrote a book titled *How Should We Then Live?* I feel that I may have left you with the same question.

As a fellow traveler, I don't have all the answers. I can't see around the next corner of my own road, let alone tell you how to navigate yours. I've discovered some tools that help me, however, and I'd like to share them with you.

Every garden or building project needs tools. Most projects can be done with quite simple tools. A shovel can turn soil for a garden or dig the foundation for a house. A hammer can be used to put together stud framework or drive the finishing nail in a fine piece of oak molding. A saw can cut tomato stakes or roof timbers. In the next three chapters I'll share three simple sets of tools with you: tools for thought-conditioning, tools for imaging, and tools for action. With these as a starting point, you can go a long way toward growing and building your life. Sure, you may want to add some rechargeable power tools to your kit in the future, but the tools discussed in these pages will get you started.

Chapter 10

Tools for Conditioning Your Thoughts

I once asked Dr. Peale which of his many books, other than the best-seller *The Power of Positive Thinking,* he thought had helped people the most. "It wasn't a book," he replied. "It was a little thirty-two-page booklet I wrote years ago called *Thought Conditioners.*

"Once I was on an airplane coming home from Chicago and a man stopped me and said, 'Dr. Peale, you saved my life!' Well, I knew that was hardly the case, but I asked him what had prompted such a dramatic statement.

"'It's this little book,' he replied, holding up a tattered copy of *Thought Conditioners*—missing a cover and held together with adhesive tape. 'This little book helped me climb out of a deep despair to which I saw no solution.'

"Seeing the poor condition of the booklet, I said, 'Here, let me have that, and I'll send you a brand-new copy.'

"'Oh, no,' he replied. 'This is the one that did the trick; I'll just hang on to it.'"

The principle behind thought-conditioning is similar to that behind air-conditioning. Just as air-conditioning changes the atmosphere of a room, keeping it fresh and healthy, thought-conditioning changes the atmosphere of your mind, giving clarity, peak health, and vitality to your life. Thought-conditioning is the first of three tools that can be used to build the spiritual framework and keep it vital and strong.

Thoughts are the basic ingredients of all phases of the inner life we've been discussing. They're the expression of the seeds of Belief, Kindness, and Optimism; they're the building blocks of solid Faith, Hope, and Love. Furthermore, they provide the energy that needs to be sent out by a pure spirit to shape and build our mental, emotional, and physical being. Without healthy, powerful thoughts providing this energy, all efforts at self-control, discipline, and change will be ineffective. Dr. Peale said it well in the introduction to his booklet:

> *Since happiness and effectiveness depend upon the kinds of thoughts we think, it is absolutely impossible to be happy if we think unhappiness-producing thoughts. If you put into your mind thoughts of fear, you will get thoughts of fear out of your mind. Fill your mind with resentment thoughts, and resentment attitude will emerge. And in neither case, of course, can you find happiness-inducing thoughts. Whatever the condition of your mind, thought-conditioning is so powerful that it can displace unhealthy thoughts. Indeed, displacement is the only way you can drive a thought from the mind.*

This technique of simultaneous displacement/replacement is the only technique that works for changing your pattern of thoughts. Whether you're trying to nurture Kindness or Optimism, energize Hope or Faith, or apply Love to your headache, you can't change your thoughts without displacement/replacement.

The reason for this is very simple: your mind is never empty. The moment you try to "empty" your mind, it attracts little bits of dust and debris that are floating around with no place to go. Who wants an empty mind anyway? What we want is a mind full of energy-producing positive thoughts. The problem, in many cases, is that we've been conditioned to dwell on the negative. Our minds get filled up and distracted with doubts, resentments, shopping lists we should have written down (and then forgotten), and worries about things over which we have no control.

Displacement works on the principle that your mind can't hold two types of thought at once. Try this simple test. For the next sixty seconds, don't think about your name. Impossible, isn't it? The minute I threw the thought of your name into your mind, it stuck there; you couldn't, no matter how hard you tried, *not* think about it. However, you could think about something else, effectively "displacing" your name. Easy. Think about your mother's name. Hard. Concentrate. See? You're no longer thinking about your own name. When you choose replacement thoughts that are high, noble, inspiring, and loving, the low, feeble, fearful, and hateful thoughts are immediately displaced, and their effect on you is minimized.

That there's power in the thoughts we think isn't a new discovery—one made by me or even Dr. Peale. I happen to believe God made us this way—powerful in thought—and that wise people have known and used this truth for thousands of years. But, like every great truth, it has to be learned by each generation. It keeps getting "lost," and then someone has to "discover" it again. Saint Paul spoke of the power of this principle when he wrote in Romans, "Be transformed by the renewing of your mind" (Rom. 12:2). Much of what I learned in seminary wasn't of practical value, but I learned something about this quote that's stayed with me for twenty-plus years. Paul originally wrote that passage in Greek, and the Greek word that we translate as *transformed* can also be translated as *metamorphosed.* In other words, we have the possibility of becoming to our old selves as a butterfly is to a caterpillar by using the power of displacing negative thoughts with positive ones that renew our minds. Here are three techniques for thought replacement:

Reading

Remember what my friend Charlie Jones says: "You're the same person today you will be five years from now except for two things: the people you meet and the books you read."

Reading is a powerful tool for adding positive thoughts to your mental processes. With the wealth of audio, video, and compact disc players joining televisions on the market, more and more people are laying aside reading for listening to books and music or, even worse, watching videos and television. Yet I'm convinced that there's a power in reading you can't get from other media. Reading takes concentration; it's active, not passive. Making a difference in your thought life takes effort. There's nothing wrong with listening or watching; it just won't do the job that reading does.

I mentioned that thought-conditioning, like air-conditioning, freshens the atmosphere. Thought-conditioning is also similar to another modern kind of conditioning: physical or strength conditioning. Everyone concerned with health is aware of the articles and books written in recent years about the benefits of aerobic and strength conditioning. Eating the right foods, sleeping the right amount, and avoiding bad substances (such as tobacco and excessive alcohol)—all these relatively passive efforts are important, but they're not enough to produce optimum health. You must exercise and condition your body through *active* efforts as well.

In the same way, you must take active effort with your mind, and that's best done through reading. No amount of listening to speeches, no amount of conversation with stimulating people—

as good as those things are—can compensate for exercising the mind through reading good books. As one literacy campaign advertisement says, "Reading is fundamental."

Perhaps I have this extra passion for reading because I'm in the publishing business. Maybe so, but the letters and calls I get about the benefits of reading good material keep me convinced. Not long ago we asked magazine subscribers to tell us their stories of how reading the inspirational material published by the Peale Center had helped them. The letters flooded in. One in particular—from a grandmother in Pennsylvania who'd been reading our material for almost forty years—stuck with me. Let me share a part of her letter with you:

> *When I read your letter and glanced around my living room, it was filled with Dr. Peale's books. There was* Enthusiasm Makes the Difference *on one end table and* The Power of Positive Living *on the other. On the mantle, amongst my treasured books, was* The Power of Positive Thinking. *I probably would have had my other favorite,* Imaging, *there too, but in doing a good deed and lending it to someone in need, it was never returned. I tried to get another copy but was told it was out of print.*
>
> *While flying to San Francisco a while back, I was reading* Imaging *and thinking about a friend's daughter. She was having some difficulty in her life, and I decided to give her the book when I got back to Pennsylvania. It must have had a good influence on her, as she got out of a bad relationship and found a very nice guy who treats her great. She now has a family with two children.*
>
> *I was first given Dr. Peale's book* The Power of Positive Thinking *by my father-in-law in the early years of my marriage. The book so inspired me that when I learned of my husband's desire to return to Penn State to earn an advanced degree, I was enthusiastic, even though those around us told us it would be impossible. You see, we*

had two young children and another one on the way. To say the least, our friends and families thought we had gone overboard when my husband quit his job and we headed off to State College, PA, with two toddlers and a two-week old baby. I had no doubt we would make it. Here are just a few of the amazing things that happened:

1. We put an ad in the paper to rent a house, but it got mixed up and placed in the "wanted to buy" column. We got so many calls from prospective sellers that one finally agreed to rent a beautiful little home we could afford with an option to buy.

2. One Saturday night my middle daughter badly needed clothes to start kindergarten, so I went down to the W. T. Grant store where we had a charge account and charged forty dollars. I didn't know why, but I wasn't worried about being able to pay the bill. The next Tuesday I got a check in the mail for forty dollars from my father. He had won some money and decided to share it with us. Why? Why do you think? That was the first and last time he sent us money.

3. Another time I was in a store admiring an appliance cart and wanted one badly because we had little counter space in our kitchen, but I knew we couldn't afford one. I decided to work on getting one, believing we could find a way, but still I didn't know how. A short time later I looked out my window and a neighbor from quite a distance was pushing an identical cart down the road toward our house. She came to our door and said she had gotten a new freezer and the cart wouldn't fit in her kitchen now, would we like to have it?

4. Imagine my joy and satisfaction in attending my husband's graduation with our children and watching with such pride as he received his master's degree and, two years later, his doctorate. The best part was that his education was completed and we didn't owe a single penny to anyone. Like Dr. Peale, I firmly believe that "all things are possible for those who believe."

Have we gotten lucky breaks, or has it been faith and positive thinking? You decide. All I know is that we always have many obstacles to overcome, but with hard work and perseverance, we come out on top.

What impresses me most about that letter is how long this grandmother has depended on the inspiration and faith she gleaned from reading, and how that faith has supported her in many everyday, down-to-earth, real-life situations. She closes the letter with thanks for all she's learned and a two-part list of what she's going to attempt next! Follow her example; get going by using good reading as the first step in thought-conditioning.

Memorization

The second great tool for thought-conditioning is memorization. Great quotations (and even whole passages) from the books you've read have the ability to sink deep into your subconscious mind and stay there, causing your entire personality to be permeated with their positive effects. Ancient cultures were much more tuned to the use of memory than we are today—initially because written words hadn't been invented and then, after they were, because writing materials were expensive and difficult to preserve. Passing memories and stories orally from generation to generation was the preferred method of communicating history, culture, laws, and principles in those early days. Even when writing and the means to record it were available, writing was often used as an aid to, rather than a substitute for, memorization.

Particularly instructive on this point is the wisdom of the ancient Jews, whose laws and customs we have recorded in the first few books of the Bible. How those laws and customs are to be applied, however, is recorded in the book of Deuteronomy: "Love the Lord your God with all your heart and with all your soul, and with all your strength. These commandments that I give you today are to be upon your hearts. Impress them on your children. Talk about them when you sit at home and when you walk along the road, when you lie down and when you get up. Tie them as symbols on your hands and bind them on your foreheads. Write them on the doorframes of your houses and on your gates" (6:5–9).

The phrase that sticks out for me in this passage (and many others like it in the Old and New Testaments of the Bible) is "upon your hearts." The concept of the heart in scripture relates generally not to the physical organ but to the spiritual center of being. The term *heart* refers to the intersection of conscious and subconscious thought. The heart is the place where the attitudes we hold overcome the veneer we put on when pressure comes into our lives. It's the place where submerged anger comes lashing out, surprising and often wounding ourselves and others. It's also the place where great deeds of good reside, awaiting the crisis moment to bring them forth. And the heart is shaped by words, thoughts, and attitudes that are held in memory.

This idea of committing great thoughts to memory is the key behind the concept of thought-conditioning as taught by Dr. Peale through the years. His booklet on the subject describes the process:

> *The process I have used both personally and in counseling, which has accomplished most impressive results, is simply that of committing these great passages to memory. One puts them in the mind as in a sort of spiritual medicine cabinet, each to be drawn out as needed for specific ills or maladies of the personality, or to meet life's situations as they develop. The method is also to conceive of these*

thoughts as having displacement value, crowding out injurious thought patterns.

The best results are gained by utilizing spare minutes to say these "thought conditioners" over and over. As you are riding on a bus or train, or washing the dishes, or waiting for an appointment, utilize fractional moments to dwell and meditate upon the meaning of these texts. As you do so, there will flash out from them new insights, new perceptions of truth. Gradually, by a deep therapy, they will drive into the mind until presently your life will become a living demonstration of God's Power.

The power and ability of memory to affect our lives is perhaps most dramatically revealed when we hear the story of someone stripped of all else but memory. One such story has deeply touched my own life, for the person involved shared my chosen profession.

At eight o'clock on the morning of Saturday, March 16, 1985, a green Mercedes sedan slowed to a stop beside journalist Terry Anderson's car in Beirut, Lebanon. Three young, bearded gunmen jumped out, grabbed Terry and pushed him into the back, and raced away. Nearly seven years passed while Terry, the former Associated Press chief Middle East correspondent, was held in captivity. Although he was moved several times, he was rarely allowed to leave the bare, windowless rooms where Shiite fundamentalists held him and other hostages.

In his book *Den of Lions,* Terry tells how he not only survived the unrelenting hardships but overcame depression and grew stronger through the power of faith and love and the tool of memory. Whether Terry was playing chess games in his mind or recalling hymns to sing in his cell, he found that the strength and depth of his memory gave him a grip on sanity and hope. When, in the late evening on Wednesday, December 4, 1991, the same green Mercedes slowed to a stop and Terry was pushed out onto the side of the road, it was only his body the fundamentalists freed; his spirit had never been captive.

Prayer

Terry Anderson's account also illustrates the presence and power of prayer as a tool for thought-conditioning. Both Terry and his waiting family recall that when all else went against them, they still had prayer—he in captivity, and they in the quest for his freedom.

The subject of spiritual interest has captured the attention of most of the major news publications and television stations in recent years. A combined study by CBS News and the Gallup organization in 1994 showed that over 90 percent of Americans pray regularly. Nearly 70 percent of us feel we've had our prayers answered at one time or another. Yet despite this focus on and acknowledgment of prayer, I believe we've just begun to rediscover the depth and breadth of its power. Prayer is, by definition, talking to God. And if you believe, as I do, that God is waiting and listening, prayer is the mightiest resource we could ever have available. Think of it: you have a hotline to the Creator and Sustainer of the universe! Why not pick it up and give God a call?

I think there are two basic reasons that we fail to use prayer as we should. First, we imagine that prayer, like the hotline during the Cold War that ran directly between the president in Washington and the premier in Moscow, is only for extreme emergencies. Nothing could be further from the truth. Those who practice prayer and find it most effective are those who use it *before* they need it desperately. Just as you can't wait to practice a fire drill in your home or office until the moment a fire breaks out, you can't get the benefit and efficacy of prayer in a crisis; it's too late.

Every year *Guideposts* magazine holds a "Family Day of Prayer" during Thanksgiving week. A couple of years ago the magazine sent a card to every family who called or wrote regarding prayer for that particular year. On the card were these simple words: "Prayer should be our first resource, not our last resort."

This is the principle that creates real power surrounding prayer: prayer is for everyone. It certainly doesn't take seminary training or clerical vows. In fact, the more "religious" people are, the greater their tendency to direct their minds toward stylized, formal, ineffective prayer. God wants to hear from us, just as a parent likes to hear from a child, and he's not a stickler for presentation.

As the father of three teenagers, I am pleased the most when my kids talk to me. When they were little, it was hard to shut them up, but I rarely wanted to; I enjoyed the interaction and even the endless questions. But now they think that they've got life figured out and that I'm a bit outdated, so there isn't much to talk to me about except the weather and sports scores. So when one of my boys sits down and asks me what I think about a news item or a person we know or a school problem, I delight in listening and responding. God is the same way. To God, we're like teenagers who think we've gotten so big that we don't need to ask him for advice or help anymore. When we take the time to sit down and talk to him, he's delighted to listen and answer.

Talk to God the way you would to a good friend. Tell God about your day; discuss ideas, decisions, and alternatives with him. When you begin to find an easy flow to this conversation, you'll find that your petitions for the needs of others and your personal requests flow easily into the conversation.

Basically, prayer has two types of results. First, I strongly believe (and have seen repeated dramatic evidence) that prayer changes things. For example, I see no other explanation than answered prayer to the physical healing that Kieran Delamere experienced. And that's just one example among many. Over and over again I've prayed for individuals, only to later learn that their situation changed for the better at an exact moment in time. You guessed it: that time coincided exactly with the time I was in prayer.

Second, prayer changes *us*. We don't always get the answer we want, but we get *an* answer. The great British writer C. S. Lewis married late in life and was deeply in love with his American wife, Joy. Within a few years, however, she contracted cancer. (Perhaps you've seen the story dramatized in the film *Shadowlands*.)

Throughout their ordeal together Lewis prayed that Joy would be healed. He was a distinguished theologian, a professor (first at Oxford and then at Cambridge), and an accomplished and celebrated author, yet his prayer wasn't answered as he'd hoped: with healing. At first Lewis was angry with God; his faith was shaken, and he cried out in anguish. As time passed, however, he saw how his praying had changed him and had helped him come through a trial experienced by many people the world over. Later he wrote the deeply moving book *A Grief Observed*, which has helped millions of people deal with the loss of a loved one. Prayer didn't change the cancer, but it did change Lewis so that he could survive and help others in a process that all must one day face.

These, then, are the tools for thought-conditioning: reading, memorization, and prayer. Used together, exercised over time and in a plan, they can help you build a framework of Faith, Hope, and Love that doesn't just survive, it succeeds. As your thoughts are conditioned, they become fresher, more vibrant.

With such renewed thinking, anything is possible, for all possibilities start with an idea.

Your thoughts become stronger as well as fresher; they become braver, less fearful, more inclined to run to possibilities instead of problems. Strong thoughts strengthen the heart that holds them, and a strong heart can handle the broken places of life we all face.

Too simple, you say? Perhaps. But since the first chapter I've held the position that finding, building, and living better through your spiritual potential *is* a simple process—simple, but not easy. If you say to me, "It can't be as simple as starting a program of memorization or reading or prayer; that's too easy," then I know where you'll end up. You won't memorize because you think that's too simple, and then the great thought you need for the crisis next month won't be there. In its absence you'll fall into an old pattern of anger, avoidance, fear, or failure.

The Chinese have a saying, "A journey of a thousand miles begins with a single step." A journey from where you are now in your spiritual ability to a stronger place begins with a first step—a step of reading, memorization, or prayer. Take that first step and the journey is begun; you're already in a better place.

Remember the fable about the king's horse? It goes something like this: "For lack of a nail the shoe was lost, for lack of a shoe the horse was lost, for lack of a horse the king was lost, for lack of a king the battle was lost, and losing the battle lost the kingdom." Simple things matter, in our lives and in our decisions.

My worst travel experience is the Los Angeles to New York "red-eye," which hurtles you through the night and puts you down in New York early the following morning. I have to take that trip several times a year and have come up with some pretty good ways to defeat the jet lag and general exhaustion of the trip.

Not long ago I was hurrying through the Los Angeles airport with just a few minutes to spare when a woman with two small children grabbed my arm and exclaimed, "Eric, Eric Fellman! Gosh, I never imagined I'd run into you in Los Angeles. How are you?"

Even looking closely at her and inventorying each kid, I didn't have a clue who the woman was. But being in a hurry, I simply put on a big smile and said, "Great! How are you and the kids?"

"Oh, we're fine. Haven't Jimmy and Mary grown up since we saw you last?"

Now I knew the kid's names, but I still had no idea who she was. I plunged ahead anyway: "Yeah, they sure have gotten big. Uh, what brings you to the airport?"

"Oh," she replied, "we just dropped George off. He's off on a trip for a week. He'll be so sorry he missed you. Is Joy with you?"

This was starting to get embarrassing. She knew Joy, I now knew her husband's and children's names, and I had live evidence in front of me, but my slow-witted brain couldn't come up with a connection. There she was, clinging to me like a long-lost friend, expecting some marvelous update on family life since we last met—and I didn't have a clue. So I did the only reasonable thing; I ducked out.

"Listen," I said, "I'm late for the flight, so I've got to run, but it was really great to see you. I'll tell Joy we ran into each other, and maybe she'll be with me next time I come out."

"Oh, that would be marvelous," she gushed. "I know Joy has our number, so you catch your plane. It was just so great to see you. Who would've thought we'd run into each other in this huge airport?"

"Incredible," I agreed. Giving her a quick hug and the kids each a pat on the head, I dashed off for my flight.

I approached the check-in counter at a trot, lugging two carry-on bags in my left hand and reaching into my coat pocket with my right to retrieve my ticket folder for the agent. Just as he took it from me, someone grabbed my overloaded left arm and the bags thudded to the floor.

"Who are you?" demanded a rather matronly woman.

"Excuse me?" I asked, not a little exasperated.

"Now wait just a minute," she replied. "I saw that woman grab onto you back there, and I know this is Los Angeles, so I just know you're some kind of celebrity. Let me have your autograph!"

By now I'd about had it with strangers grabbing my arm, so I said, "Look, lady, I'm not anybody whose autograph means anything. You have me confused with someone else."

"You don't have to get so uppity," she replied. "It wouldn't hurt you to give out a couple of autographs. Here, just sign the back of my ticket envelope. I even have a pen handy."

By this time a few other people were watching, so I wanted out of the situation as quickly as possible. Seeing her determined stare, I gave in; I started to scribble something illegible on her ticket envelope. Just then the agent for my flight said to me, "Okay, Mr. Fellman, seat 26B on the exit row is all set for you." Whereupon the woman snarled, "What? Why you *aren't* anybody, are you!"

With that she grabbed the pen and ticket envelope back and went off in a huff. Ten or twelve strangers standing around us began to laugh. A few minutes later, as I was boarding the plane, a fellow traveler reached out for me and said, in mocking tones, "Why, who are you, anyway?" and then roared with laughter. By the time I found my seat, I was thoroughly humiliated and thought everyone was snickering at me.

Usually such an experience would ruin my whole day. The previous week hadn't gone all that well, and now I'd been embarrassed at the airport by first forgetting a friend's name (and very existence!) on the one hand and being rejected by a total stranger on the other. The stranger's words, "You *aren't* anybody, are you!" echoed in my mind.

I was several months into a memorization program at this point, and these lines of a favorite poem—"If," by Rudyard Kipling—came into my mind:

If you can meet with Triumph and Disaster
and treat those two impostors just the same;
Or watch the things you gave your life to broken,
And stoop to build 'em up with worn-out tools . . .

If you can fill the unforgiving minute
With sixty seconds' worth of distance run,
Yours is the Earth and everything that's in it,
And—which is more—you'll be a man my son.

The power of those words bubbled up from my mind, refreshed my spirit, and led me to the next exercise. I simply whispered a prayer for those two women. One prayer was for the unknown friend and her two children to get home safely and for George to get back to them at the end of the week. (And you know, hard as we tried, Joy and I never did come up with their last name and identity.) My other prayer was for the stranger, that she would find someone in all of Los Angeles worthy of her autograph collection. Those two exercises, the memory work and the prayer, changed the tone of my six-hour flight. In fact, I started thinking, on that flight, that I should write down some of these experiences so that someday they could go into a book. And hey, six-hour flights are usually nice and quiet for writing, aren't they?

Key Discoveries

Preparation

We've looked at three tools for thought-conditioning: reading, memorization, and prayer. These tools can be used to cultivate the seeds of your spirituality, build your inner spiritual framework, and strengthen the outer planes of your life. Here are some further suggestions to get you started:

Action

1. *Reading:* Make a list of four inspirational books or magazines you want to read. Get out your planning calendar and make a schedule for reading them cover to cover. Need a suggestion? Try any book in the New Testament; *Love, Medicine, and Miracles,* by Bernie Siegel; or *Healing and the Mind,* by Bill Moyers.
2. *Memorization:* Highlight passages in the reading material you cover above, and commit the key ones to memory.
3. *Prayer:* Find a regular time each day to try talking to God in regular, everyday words for just ten minutes. Then allow yourself another few minutes of silence in order to listen for answers. When you have this habit established, move ahead with shooting "flash" prayers to God about anything and everything that happens during your day. Use so-called wasted time—for example, time spent waiting for buses or elevators or sitting in the toll lane on the freeway—for this activity. Begin to imagine God beside you all day long, listening and advising like a good friend. Then you can quit imagining. God is there.

Chapter 11

Tools for Imaging

Imaging, sometimes called *visualization,* is the forming of complete, detailed mental pictures of life situations. When formed in combination with spiritual resources, these pictures develop a purity and clarity that help them sink deep into the unconscious mind, where they create an energy that empowers the person to obtain and use resources far beyond what would normally be available.

This concept was one of Dr. Peale's most deeply held and widely taught techniques of positive thinking. It was the subject of several individual conversations I had with him. He also wrote an entire book—*Positive Imaging*—on the subject. Let me share his definition of imaging from the opening chapter of that book:

> *Imaging is positive thinking carried one step further. In imaging, one does not merely think about a hoped-for goal; one "sees" or visualizes it with tremendous intensity, reinforced by prayer. Imaging is a kind of laser beam of the imagination, a shaft of mental energy in which the desired goal or outcome is pictured so vividly by the conscious mind that the unconscious mind accepts it and is activated by it. This releases powerful internal forces that can bring about astonishing changes in the life of the person who is doing the imaging.*

Peale was repeatedly and excessively criticized by conservative religious commentators for his belief in and support of imaging.

As imaging (and its counterpart, visualization) spread, increasingly adopted by doctors, psychiatrists, athletes, and others, these commentators warned that it was a "secular" technique and somehow tainted and unfit for spiritual use. Then, during a firestorm of controversy that pitted established religions against "new" religions, imaging became associated with cults, mysticism, and witchcraft. Soon anyone who used this technique was labeled "New Age" or "satanic." Dr. Peale took a lot of heat, and I often asked him about the controversy.

"I find the logic of these arguments ridiculous, Eric," he said to me once. "Because a crime figure drives a car, does driving a car make me a criminal? No, of course not. Let's put the same sort of argument in spiritual terms. Every religion espouses some type of prayer. In my world travels I've seen prayer mats, prayer wheels, prayer ladders, and prayer vigils. Satan worshipers pray to Satan. Does that mean I should stop praying to Jesus? No, of course not.

"I use a simple test to decide if a technique is proper or not. I just ask the question, 'What did Jesus say?' In this case the answer is recorded in Mark 11:24: 'Therefore, I tell you whatever you ask for in prayer, believe that you have received it, and it will be yours.'"

Since that conversation I've applied Dr. Peale's test to the issue of imaging. The results? Visions and dreams that became reality flow through the Bible from beginning to end. The New Testament is filled with references similar to the one Dr. Peale cited to me that day. You might look, for example, at Matthew 7:7, Matthew 21:22, James 1:5–6, and 1 John 5:14. Each teaches a simple formula of first believing in something enough to pray for it and then believing that the prayer has been answered enough to act on the result.

These principles have become a three-part formula for imaging that's taught throughout the publications and seminars of the

Peale Center. The formula is visualize, prayerize, actualize. As we begin an examination of this formula, let me share a true story that's an amazing illustration of the power of this plan.

About twenty-five years ago, a boy of eighteen boarded an airplane in Seoul, South Korea, bound for the United States and his college education. As he looked out the window before the plane pulled back from the gate, he could see his family—mother, father, brother, sisters, cousins, aunts, and uncles—standing there watching him leave. Yun Kul Cheung (Y. K.) had never felt so alone. But the hopes and dreams of his family were spurring him on; he was determined not to fail.

Struggling through his first year of college, Y. K. found an aptitude for business and accounting. He began to settle in to the United States and soon fell in love with its diverse cultures and unlimited opportunities. Compared with the rigid rules in his Korean homeland, America was truly the land of opportunity. It wasn't surprising, then, that after graduation and returning home, Y. K. would set his sights on returning to the United States.

First some obligations had to be met at home, however; and while Y. K. was tackling those obligations, love began to grow. Never losing sight of his goal, Y. K. worked hard to repay his family and married his lovely fiancée, Helen. Having never left South Korea, she found it hard to think of moving to America, but because she believed in the dreams of her husband, the couple soon returned to the Los Angeles area. With his skills in accounting and his ability to relate with and understand immigrants, he soon landed a job with an accounting firm handling cross-cultural accounts. But Y. K. had a dream beyond simply working for a big company; he wanted to be successful on his own. He kept his eyes and his mind open for opportunities, and soon several observations led to an experiment that would prove to be the beginning of an amazing accomplishment.

Living in an area of ethnic neighborhoods, Y. K. noticed that many immigrants didn't trust banks, and in return many banks didn't trust immigrants. This meant that workers had a difficult time cashing checks. Banks often questioned whether funds would be available to support checks presented by immigrants who, because of their distrust, had no bank account. But Y. K. knew that the immigrants were fiercely independent and determined to succeed. Rather than being a poor risk, they were a great risk. They would work extra hours, skip meals, and take on second jobs in order to be successful. So, with a bit of cash from his wife's flower business, Y. K. opened storefront check-cashing stations in ethnic neighborhoods. The concept was an instant success. For a fee he would cash the checks and provide money orders and other services. True to his belief, his customers rarely tried to cheat him with bad checks, and the business grew rapidly.

Now his big dream began to take shape. As trust developed between Y. K. and his customers, he thought, "Why not try to establish a neighborhood thrift and loan association and teach my customers the importance of earning interest and having a place to get small loans?" No major banking or thrift institution in the entire Los Angeles area would even consider such an idea. Why, immigrants had no credit, didn't own houses for collateral, and were constantly on the move. Once again, Y. K. knew what others did not: that the people who were his customers would do anything to prove themselves, avoid confrontation, and earn their citizenship.

However, starting a thrift and loan isn't a small proposition in the best of times, and Y. K. was dreaming his dream in the middle of the savings and loan crisis in the late 1980s. Not only did he face myriad state and federal banking regulations, but to top it off he had to have two and a half million dollars cash as working capital before he could open the doors of a thrift and loan.

When he was in college, Y. K. had been given the book *The Power of Positive Thinking*, and he'd been so inspired by that book that he now decided to write to the author about his dream. Dr. Peale shared Y. K.'s letter with me, as well as his reply, which encouraged the young man to use imaging principles and work toward the dream. On my next trip to California, I gave Y. K. a call, and we became friends. That gave me the privilege of following him as he used the tools of visualizing, prayerizing, and actualizing (and of watching the amazing results).

The first major hurdle was a bureaucratic one. In order to be enrolled in the approval process, he had to demonstrate a need for his thrift and loan concept. This meant getting valid signatures from ten thousand people willing to say that they felt the institution was needed in their community. This wasn't easy for Y. K., even among his customers, for they remained cynical about banks in general. They had his storefront locations to cash their checks, they tried to stay out of debt, and they could go to "private lenders" (read "loan sharks") when they were in exceptional need of money. Finally Y. K. stood on street corners with his petition and this message: "Look, friends, this is America. Don't you think I should be given the right to try this crazy scheme?" He got his ten thousand names off patriotism.

The next hurdle was the one I never thought he could jump—the two and a half million dollars. Y. K. had only about thirty thousand dollars of his own money. He put that in a holding account for safekeeping until he had enough. Then he began to visualize the account having the full amount. First he took out a blank check for the account and wrote, "$2,500,000 and no/100," to be paid to the order of L.A. Thrift and Loan—the name he had chosen to use. Y. K. took that check and propped it up on his desk. He looked at it every morning and evening. Then he took the second step: he "prayerized" over the check. After several weeks another idea came to him. Making a list of every business acquaintance and friend he could think of, he began to guess how much they might invest in his thrift and loan, if they could be convinced. He listed the amounts and then went a step further. He photocopied a standard blank check form and made facsimile checks for the estimated amounts. He took this stack of pretend checks and counted them every evening. After a few more weeks the total came to two and a half million. Now Y. K. took the last step: he actualized his dream. Armed with his prospectus, his vision, and the pretend checks, he began to call on the people on his list.

During this time we talked often on the telephone, and always Y. K. had news of another confirmed investor or a request that I pray for an appointment he had scheduled with a tentative investor. After a while I stopped doubting him, so I wasn't surprised when he called to say that the total was on deposit in the holding account. There were still months of bureaucratic red tape ahead, and more visualizing, prayerizing, and actualizing with countless officials whose approval had to be earned, but in October of 1990, L.A. Thrift and Loan opened its doors. Eric and Joy Fellman were the first depositors, with a certificate of deposit of five thousand dollars (which paid, I might add, 7.2 percent). Never have I seen a more potent example of visualization and its power to make a dream come true.

Let's take an in-depth look at these three tools: visualizing, prayerizing, and actualizing.

Visualizing

The technique of creating a clear mental image of the desired result is a skill that must be practiced. Most of us feel foolish when we first sit down to try this technique. We get stalled with thoughts like these: "How do I know this idea is the right one?" "Who am I to think I could ever gain an investor's confidence?" For me it was this: "So many books have already been written by better writers with more education. Why should anyone want to read what I write?" The answer, in every case, is that it takes courage to overcome feelings of foolishness and self-doubt.

Courage is the ingredient that allows you to picture *even a foolish idea,* to believe in it when no one else seems to be listening. That's how Henry Ford created a market for cars when everyone else said horses would never go out of fashion. That's how Thomas Edison started an entertainment empire and founded a whole new industry out of moving pictures when everyone else said they'd be nothing more than a fad novelty used in nickel picture shows.

It doesn't take much courage to start picturing a brighter future—just the courage to look silly. If even that's hard, start small. I couldn't imagine 250 pages of a book manuscript being finished, but I could imagine 20 pages of a chapter. So I took out 20 sheets of white paper, put a title on the first page, and looked at the stack, picturing the pages full of words and ideas. It was courage that let Kieran Delamere tell the doctors he was going to walk, even when they could show him scientifically that it was impossible. Courage is a lot easier when supported by faith, which is why having a strong spiritual framework is so important to accomplishment in any area of life. The key that frees your mind to see the good outcome is courage, and faith in God inspires a lot of courage you wouldn't have otherwise.

Once you've begun practicing creating a mental picture of a good outcome, it helps tremendously to put something down on paper or to make some other physical representation of the vision. Y. K. Cheung wrote out pretend checks; a couple whom Joy and I know well cut out pictures of dream houses they wanted to build, so when it came time to sit down with the architect they had a folder full of ideas for kitchens, bathrooms, overall floor plans, and landscaping.

Finally—and this is key—you must practice your visualization technique on a regular basis. It does no good to create and hold one picture for one day. You must repeat the process on a daily basis in order that the mental picture forms so powerfully that its energy can begin to flow through you to completion.

Prayerizing

With the tool of prayerizing you fully and completely cover your mental picture with prayer. This prayer tool performs two vital functions. First, when your idea is presented to the Almighty, you discover that God loves ideas, creativity, and vision. God also often has a better idea, so taking your wishes, hopes, and aspirations to God makes them better. Y. K. Cheung often told me that it was the time he spent in prayer that gave him each new idea for moving his thrift and loan project forward. Once there was such resistance from an official in the California state offices in Sacramento that Y. K. was beside himself regarding a solution, yet he continued to pray each morning for this person. One morning he came out of his prayer time with the distinct feeling he should drop everything, drive to Sacramento, and see the man. He listened to his inner voice, and when he arrived at the office the man said, "Well, I was going to deny this application because you have listed as your chairman a foreign citizen [a Korean businessman looking for U.S. investments]. But if you want to explain to me another arrangement, I'll give you an extension."

Y. K. was able to work out the situation much more quickly in person than he would have been if he'd been slapped with a denial and had had to start all over at the beginning.

The first thing prayerizing an idea does is put God's energy into the endeavor. Because God works through you, you get his energy into your idea. The second thing prayerizing does is change you. Every one of us has aspects of our lives that need adjusting and correcting. Sometimes the greatest hindrance to the accomplishment we envision is ourselves. My tennis hero, Jimmy Connors, plateaued early in his career due to his terrible temper. He could get only so far before his temper would boil over; he would then either lose the game or lose his temper with officials (which was in some ways worse for his career). Once Jimmy got a handle on his temper, however, the rest was history-making tennis.

Taking our fondest dreams to God in prayer causes us to stand before the Almighty and feel his fond assistance, but it also makes us aware, sometimes painfully, of the grit and grime in our own lives. It's this contact with God that allows us to be cleansed. Sometimes it's a wrong we've done another person that needs to be righted. Sometimes it's a fear that needs to be unveiled and overcome. Whatever the source of the grit in our lives, prayer will wash it out and make us ready to function at maximum potential.

Once we're cleansed, prayer delivers power into our ideas and actions. Earlier in this book I described the outlook of Sir John Marks Templeton, one of the fathers of modern mutual fund investing. A deeply spiritual person, Sir John is also the founder of the Templeton Prize for Religion, an award rivaling the Nobel Prize in significance and impact. Each year an individual who has contributed greatly to the advancement of the understanding of God and spirituality in the world is awarded a sum just over one million dollars to further his or her work.

At a breakfast interview I was conducting for *PLUS* magazine one day, I asked Sir John to tell me the key to his success.

"Backed by our beliefs," he said, "we're not so uptight and on edge as those who are in the business merely to make money. We start each day by setting our minds on important things and praying. All our transactions are influenced by that."

Indeed, every director and shareholder meeting Sir John leads is opened with prayer. But prayer is never used in making specific stock selections. "That would be a gross misinterpretation of God's methods," says Templeton. "What we pray for is wisdom. We pray that the decisions we make today will be wise decisions and that our talks about different stocks will be wise talks. Of course, our discussions and decisions are fallible and sometimes flawed. No one should expect that, just because he begins with prayer, every decision he makes is going to be profitable. However, I do believe that, if you pray, you will make fewer stupid mistakes."

The tool of prayer is behind some of the world's greatest political, business, and personal choices and careers. Both visualization and prayer must be followed by the tool of actualization, however.

Actualizing

The next chapter is devoted to a full discussion of this important tool for spiritual and personal development. I want to introduce it here, however, and then share a story that's been fifty years in the making. It dramatically illustrates the principle of actualization.

Once you've visualized a good outcome and placed the matter in God's care through prayer, you have to *do* something. Many people get stuck right here. They dream and they pray—and then they wait for something to happen. It reminds me of the saying, "Life is what happens while you're making other plans."

A couple of other corny clichés also come to mind: "Success is 90 percent sweat." "If at first you don't succeed, try, try again." "It's always too soon to quit." Every great athlete spends far more time practicing than playing; the ratio is something like ten or twenty to one. It's those repeated hours of effort, that practice that won't relent until the amazing move becomes second nature, that yields winning performances. Thomas Edison was perhaps the greatest inventive genius of this century. Yet when he was perfecting the lightbulb, he failed nearly five thousand times before he found a filament material that could last beyond a few minutes. Several other scientists were working on the same theory and the same experiments as Edison, at the same time. One of them even tried several hundred filaments before giving up. The only thing that made Edison the "genius" who succeeded was his dogged determination to keep trying, to test not hundreds but thousands of filaments.

Now for my story that took fifty years to develop. About half a century ago, Norman Vincent Peale and a couple of friends started *Guideposts* magazine. Its goal was to tell first-person stories of faith to inspire readers to live a faith-filled lifestyle. Having established a nonprofit organization, they raised a few donations, put together the first magazine (on the Peale kitchen table), and worked on getting it distributed. Things clunked along in this low-key fashion for a while. Then the organizers realized that, although they had about forty thousand subscribers, the income wasn't equaling the expenses. The group was faced with a fiscal crisis.

They did what every organization does in a crisis: they called a meeting. To this meeting they invited an able businesswoman named Tessie Durlock. While her brains were respected, so was her pocketbook, for she had made a rather substantial donation to the founding of *Guideposts* magazine. As Dr. Peale used to tell it, the group "was hoping lightning might strike twice."

So the meeting was convened, and Tessie sat there listening to the dismal reports of printing costs, postage costs, promotion costs, and the difficulty of finding a system for efficiently tracking forty thousand subscribers (this was long before modern computers). Finally she could take all the negative thinking no longer and exclaimed, "Norman, whatever happened to positive thinking? We've been sitting here for almost an hour, and all I've heard is what factors are against us and what we lack. We lack subscribers, we lack equipment, we lack capital—nothing but lack, lack, lack. And not one word of prayer either, just more and more negativism."

By now she had their attention, if for no other reason than that she'd shamed them into listening. "I'll bet you asked me here hoping I'd make another financial contribution to this lack-filled effort." Seeing the sheepish looks around the table, she smiled sweetly and then declared, "Well, I'm not going to do it. I'm going to work on changing your thinking, which will be much better for you.

"Norman," she continued, "you tell me there are forty thousand subscribers, but you claim that that isn't enough. Well, tell me, how many subscribers would it take to make *Guideposts* a smashing success?"

Dr. Peale thought on that for a while and decided to reach for the stars: "If we had a hundred thousand subscribers, our troubles would be over."

"All right," said Tessie, "we need a hundred thousand subscribers. Let's picture them in our minds. Look out there. Can you see them?"

For a while everyone looked at her blankly. When they saw that she'd closed her eyes to concentrate, they realized she was serious. So powerful was her example that one by one those around the table began to see the hundred thousand people. Then, to the group's surprise, Tessie said, "Okay, now that we see them, we have them. Let's pray and thank the Lord that he's given us one hundred thousand subscribers."

To the astonishment of the group, she did indeed begin praying. She asked the Lord for nothing but instead thanked him for everything in advance, including the hundred thousand subscribers. In the course of her prayer she quoted that great scriptural passage, ". . . Whatever you ask for in prayer, believe that you have received it, and it will be yours" (Mark 11:24).

In Dr. Peale's frequent retelling of this story, when Tessie hit "Amen," he opened one eye expecting to see that the pile of bills to be paid had disappeared. "But," he would say, "I soon remembered that when the Lord wants to change a situation, he has a better method. He changes people, and changed people change situations."

That's what happened. The discouraged group went from hoping for a bail-out donation to throwing out new ideas at a rapid rate. Many of the suggestions were impossible, of course, but some were great. Then the group took the final step: they got up from the table and implemented two of the ideas right away. One of these—that of writing to subscribers to ask if they'd like to give a gift subscription to a friend or relative—worked so well that soon the subscriber base had doubled; in fact, within eighteen months it stood at one hundred thousand.

Here's the rest of the story. In the late 1940s, when this meeting took place, incredible, unbelievable, stupendous success was seen as one hundred thousand subscribers. Yet in 1995, on its fiftieth birthday, *Guideposts* had not one, two, five, or even nine hundred thousand subscribers; it had four and a quarter million. The simple techniques of visualizing, prayerizing, and actualizing had produced a result forty-two and a half times greater than even the most optimistic wishes could conceive.

This is one of the most striking examples I've ever witnessed of the principle of abundance. When your spiritual framework is balanced and in control of your outward life, it keeps you in tune with the incredible power of God. The practical results are, as Saint Paul once said, ". . . Immeasurably more than all we ask or imagine," (Eph. 3:20, NIV). Truly, we have not because we ask not, and we ask not because we don't take the time to visualize and focus the object of our desires and then commit that object to prayer and action.

Key Discoveries

Preparation

This chapter has been about the incredible tools that are available to us through imaging, which is the process of creating a vivid mental picture of a desired outcome, then praying for wisdom to produce that outcome and taking action toward the goal. Those imaging tools are visualizing, prayerizing, actualizing.

Action

1. In order to create the climate for good visualization of an accurate mental picture, you must practice some of the principles of solitude. Find a quiet place and sit. Spend a few minutes relaxing. Think of yourself as a log and then as a limp, wet leaf on that log. Relax completely and then focus your mind, still in quietness, on the picture you wish to create. Once you have it, mentally "save" it as if to the hard drive of your memory, and then come back to it over and over. Once you've created the image in solitude, you should be able to call it back to memory even while walking on a crowded street or while driving your car. Work on the image over and over until it becomes rooted in your unconscious mind.

2. Next, prayerize the visualization you've pictured. Like Sir John Templeton, pray not for specifics in the picture but for the wisdom and knowledge to make the right decisions to create the reality. Like Tessie Durlock, don't ask God for anything; instead, thank God for what he's about to supply.

3. Now you must actualize your goal. Read the next chapter and follow its procedures for a proven method of moving from idea to action.

Chapter 12

Tools for Action

A great method for moving from idea to action is summed up in the three words of a famous Nike footwear commercial: "Just do it!"

There's a great visual image in one of the teaching passages written by Saint Paul to the Ephesian church. Paul describes in great detail the "armor" that a believer dons to do battle with inner conflicts and outside influences of evil. In the military language of the day, he talks about a sword, shield, breastplate, and helmet. Then, in a curious phrase in the middle of this discourse, he says, ". . . and having done all, to stand. Stand therefore . . . " (Eph. 6:11–14, KJV). Throughout my childhood I heard sermons on this famous passage. Each piece of armor was examined in great detail, both literally and metaphorically. Modern equivalents were used as examples. The importance of protecting the feet, head, and chest was analyzed. In Sunday school we cut up cardboard boxes and made the swords, shields, and helmets for use in skits. But not once in all that time did I hear a sermon on the phrase that jumped out at me.

To me, Saint Paul's point is that once you've done all the thinking and all the praying, once all the emotions are in place, and once your framework of Faith, Hope, and Love is strong enough, get on with it. Having done everything preliminary to standing, stand up! As the commercial says, "Just do it."

Tom Peters, in his best-selling books on what makes great companies, lists one factor that characterizes all highly successful companies, whether they're deliberately in search of excellence or are thriving on chaos; these companies have a "bias for action." In other words, if faced with a situation where action is indicated but not all the facts are in, these companies take the action instead of waiting for more facts. This bias is suggested in clichés such as, "It's easier to steer a moving ship," "If at first you don't succeed, try, try again," and my personal favorite, "It's easier to gain forgiveness than permission." In every job I've ever held, I've gotten into more hot water for doing nothing than for doing something that turned out to be the wrong thing.

I learned this lesson the hard way when, at twenty-eight years old, I was placed in charge of a pretty substantial consumer magazine. Balancing the editorial, circulation, ad sales, and production concerns was heady but nerve-racking stuff. If we published the wrong article, subscribers would cancel. If we went with the wrong mailing, no new subscribers would be forthcoming. If we didn't garner enough ads, we had to cut editorial space as well. If we missed printing deadlines, the magazine was late.

One of the things the organization I worked for at that time did to control costs was buy their own paper. They had a school and book division as well as the magazine, and buying two or three train carloads of paper could sometimes deliver substantial savings. On the flip side, however, the paper market was volatile. Rising paper costs could mean either that you should buy ahead (stockpiling against a further run up) or that you should sell some excess paper you'd purchased at a lower price (thereby making a profit from the rising price before it plummeted again). Trying to manage this process once left me with an excess carload of top-quality paper. Trying to decide whether to sell or hold as the prices rose, I constantly asked the production manager for more information and for his opinion on which course we should take. He was an old salt, the kind who would always say, "Well, we *could* sell; on the other hand, we could hold it a few days." The decision was mine, and I found I couldn't make it until the bottom dropped out of the market a few days later. Before we found a buyer, twenty-five thousand dollars had been lost on that one carload. I started to learn the "just do it" principle.

Having a bias for action simply means taking the first step toward the changes you want in your life or the hopes you dream about. Each of us has the inner spiritual framework of Faith, Hope, and Love, and that framework supports, shapes, and controls the outer planes of our mental, emotional, and physical lives. The wonder of infinite variety in human beings is displayed in the multiplicity of shapes this individual life pyramid can take. None of us is ever totally in balance, as I've stressed throughout. The element of Love may be stronger in you than it is in me; your emotional being may be defined along the sides by Love and Faith and supported from behind by Hope, while mine may be defined by Faith and Hope and supported from behind by Love.

Most people spend way too much time worrying about and identifying which piece of the framework is weakest and then trying to strengthen that area and adjust the fit of the external planes. Once they've recognized the need to build and balance the framework, the actual construction work (and remodeling) sometimes becomes a lifetime process. Going to the psychiatrist, psychologist, or priest to measure the frame and sides becomes a huge element in some people's lives. A lot of time and energy is wasted in this way, since the best kind of life is found by knowing who you are and then just living.

Please don't misunderstand me. Many people are chronically unable to function well in the world and need help both in finding out where they're most out of shape and in pulling life together; they should seek that help and then begin living. Likewise, sometimes a critical situation comes along—perhaps the death of a loved one or a serious illness—that takes an otherwise able person beyond the point he or she can handle alone.

Just before I got this chapter ready to send to the publisher, the "Blizzard of 1996" hit the East Coast, including the little town where we live. I had taken the day off from the office and was putting the final touches on the manuscript. Joy and I took a break at noon to go out and get some groceries before the storm reached full fury. While we were out, the temperature dropped significantly and a water pipe burst in our basement. By the time we got home three inches of water covered the laundry and rec room floors. Immediately I did two things. First I shut off the main water supply. Next I called a plumber, because almost everything I know about plumbing is how to shut off the main water supply. No amount of thinking, imaging, praying, or acting could have allowed me to fix the problem. I needed professional help.

But this was an urgent, unusual situation. Despite the humility displayed in the previous paragraph, I *do* know how to change a faucet washer, clean a drain trap, and plunge out the commode. For those everyday problems I don't call a plumber.

I think most of us have similar abilities in life. Once you've worked on building your spiritual framework, focused your spiritual center, and begun using the tools necessary to maximize your strengths, stop working on life and live. I guess what I'm trying to say is that I've seen a lot of people waste a good portion of their lives worrying about who they *aren't* rather than making the most of who they *are.* Let me suggest two tools that are extremely useful in taking action with your life.

Setting Goals

Earlier we discussed Kenneth Blanchard's SMART outline for goals. (Remember, goals must be specific, motivational, attainable, relevant, and trackable.) However, as often as I've shared this method, I've gotten a response similar to that given to Dr. Bernie Siegel: "You've told me *what* to do, but you haven't told me *how* to do it." In other words, goals are important, but how do we set them?

To answer that question, we first have to understand what a goal is. In every one of the million books on goal setting (okay, okay, there are only 789,253), there's a different definition. Here's one that works for me, because it's simple, memorable, and workable: A *goal is a dream with a deadline.* A lot is said in those few words. Let's examine them more closely.

First, your goals should be driven by your dreams. Therein lies a key to why your spiritual framework must be in place and your external being in balance. If your spiritual framework is ignored or out of balance, your dreams will be unfocused (or worse yet, make no sense). Dreams have to start somewhere, and if your mental life is flabby because you've never thought-conditioned your mind, your dreams have nowhere to begin.

However, once you have your inner elements well balanced and able to shape your outer being, your dreams take focus. Let me share a little known result of recognizing and growing your spiritual potential. Once you find your place within God's plan, you discover that he wants you to enjoy life; therefore, goals focus on dreams. Jesus said, "I am come that they might have life, and that they might have it more abundantly." (John 10:10, KJV). Elsewhere he said, ". . . the Father will give you whatever you ask in my name." (John 14:13). That's the stuff dreams are made of. I can't ask, in Jesus' name, for utter, crushing defeat of my opponents, because he simply doesn't think like that. I *can* ask that all of my potential be realized in each opportunity. Since most of us use so little of our full potential, the results from such a request are amazing!

The second part of my "dream with a deadline" definition is, of course, the deadline. Not one chapter of this book got completed until a friend, who eventually put me in touch with an agent who found the publisher, told me she didn't want to hear about the book one more time until I could show her a chapter. I said, "Fine, I'll have it done by Memorial Day." Once I said that, the challenge to my male psyche was so great that I finished fifteen days early. That was after talking about it for eight years!

Once you understand what a goal is, there are four other "how" steps:

1. *Write the goal down.* After formulating your goal using the SMART method, record it in a place you'll look every day.
2. *Put it on the calendar.* I don't mean just set a deadline. Write it on the calendar you use to plan vacations, keep track of birthdays, and remember dental appointments.
3. *Measure your progress.* Tom Haggai, CEO of the four-billion-dollar IGA food enterprise, once told me that he never lost much weight, despite a lifetime of dieting, until he began to write down his weight each week. When he knew the measuring day was coming, his performance improved.
4. *Adjust as necessary.* Don't keep a goal you never reach. Likewise, don't keep one you reach too easily. Lower the first and raise the second.

If you follow these simple, practical steps, you'll create goals that take you places you've dreamed about but haven't been. Better yet, when you get there, you'll see places you've never even dreamed of.

Through this process you'll find those one or two goals that will drive the rest of your life, giving you purpose, meaning, fulfillment, happiness, joy, pain, heartache, frustration, and discouragement—in other words, all the great stuff in life. Sometimes this goal discovery process takes us places we'd never thought to go.

I have a friend who's a Baptist minister in the South. Through processes similar to those we've been discussing, he found a life goal of helping helpless people. His church grew, and the passion of the congregation followed his. Homeless people were given shelter, orphans found families, jobless people were trained, prisoners were visited, and hungry people were fed. One night he was praying and asking God to take him even further on this exciting, fulfilling journey. "Don't ever forget to be careful what you pray for," he jokingly says today, looking back on that night. "God just might give it to you."

What God gave was a phone call within minutes from a friend and parishioner we'll call Jake. "I'm at the doctor's office," Jake said. "He tells me I'm quite sick. Can you come down and be with me?"

Arriving at the medical building, my friend found Jake sitting outside. Looking up with tired and frightened eyes, he said simply, "I have AIDS."

The news hit my preacher friend hard. Like many conservatives, he thought AIDS was a disease that hit mainly homosexual men who weren't careful with their sex lives. He saw homosexuality as a sin, and AIDS, since it's transmitted primarily by sexual activity, as a "disease of choice."

"In other words," he said, "I had warned about this disease from the pulpit, saying how it was something that could be avoided, unlike breast cancer or leukemia. But I had never met anyone who had the disease, and Jake was a friend, a good friend.

"What I learned in that instant of shock was that I could preach against a disease all day long, but I couldn't preach against my friend. He was sick. Jesus would want me to care for him."

What followed next created a firestorm in the church. Many people couldn't understand how the preacher could "condone" Jake's sinful activity. But my minister friend, focused internally and balanced externally, weathered the storm. His attitudes and opinions were shaken, but not his faith. He saw that it was possible to fight disease, disagree about lifestyles, debate cause and effect, and all the while care for the sick in a loving fashion. Today his church is an example of a community of faith that holds its beliefs while ministering to the neediest of people. The care program for AIDS patients in their church is a model followed across the country, and it's changing how his particular branch of religion deals with people who are hurting.

Setting Priorities

Once you've learned to set goals and work on them, sooner or later setting priorities will become a problem. Surprisingly, priorities are actually harder to determine when you're focused spiritually and your life is in good balance than they are when your life is in turmoil. Before you've improved your spiritual focus—and thereby your life balance—the priorities you have to deal with are often between good and bad things, between what's clearly positive and what's clearly negative. Once focus and balance are increased, however, your choices get harder, because they're between the better and the best. Now everything you look at seems wonderful (or at least filled with potential). How can you possibly choose?

One of my lifetime friends, and a mentor from whom I've learned some of life's best principles, is Dr. George Sweeting, chancellor of Moody Bible Institute. On this subject of priorities, he says, "The main thing is remembering to keep the main thing the main thing." But how do you decide what *is* the main thing? Sweeting would say, "Remember to focus. It's better to say, 'This one thing I do' than 'These twenty-seven things I dabble in.'" Okay, Doc, but *how* do I find the one thing? He has one last piece of advice: "People, prayer, and practice."

- *People:* Cultivate mentor relationships with people you see as successful. A mentor should be someone you can (and will) trust with your biggest dreams and your biggest failures. A mentor should probably be older, certainly wiser, and definitely accessible.

- *Prayer:* Ask God what he thinks. God isn't in the business of hiding good things, as in an Easter egg hunt. God is waiting to hear from you. He won't force himself on you, but if you ask, God will answer. Be sure to listen to the answer, though. One friend of mine rushed out of her apartment late for work one cold morning to find the car dead. She kept praying, "God, please help me, please help me," but still the car didn't start. She finally went back into the apartment, where the phone had been ringing and ringing. It was her mother with vital news. God *had* been helping: he kept the car from starting so that she could get the phone call.

- *Practice:* When I first decided I wanted to try preaching, I was horrible. But I liked the experience and the potential, so I practiced.

(Pity the poor congregations I practiced on!) I'll never forget the first time I was invited *back* to preach somewhere. The practice had paid off.

When people, prayer, and practice pay off, you've found a top priority. If after using the three P's you still find yourself with too many priorities, try the Jimmy Connors method. (Well, it really isn't *his* method; I just came up with it while watching him play one time.)

In tennis they play "rounds." All the players start out playing one match, but only the winners of those initial matches advance. So thirty-two players become sixteen, and sixteen become eight, and eight become four, and four become two—and then one person wins. At a Jimmy Connors match I attended once, a chart was posted showing this "ladder" system. It's reproduced without names below.

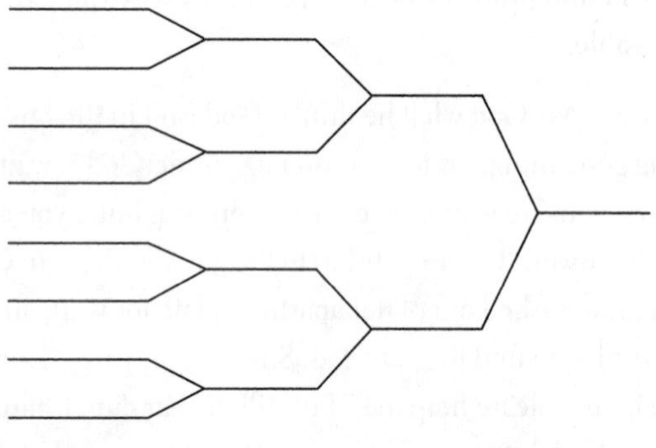

During a pause in the match, I wondered whether this tennis "ladder" could be used to prioritize ideas. I thought about it a good deal and then put it into practice, and it works. Line up your top eight or ten priorities at the wide end of the ladder, matching them in pairs, and then go through each pair and choose only one. You may have to play a "game" to decide, such as lining up the pros and cons on a piece of paper or using the people, prayer, and practice system. After repeated narrowing down, eventually only one choice is left standing. That becomes your number-one priority. If you're doubtful of the result you get, you can scramble the lineup at the beginning and run the matches again to see which idea wins. Or you can take all the losers and run the matches to find the second priority. Either way, you've forced yourself to make a commitment. As long as you write it, calendar it, measure it, and adjust it, you can't go wrong, and you *can* go very, very right. Some things are just more important than others.

A few years ago my brother and I took Father and his five grandsons on a massive canoe trip. Some of the boys were pretty little, so we didn't plan to go far and we took a lot of stuff with us. In fact, we used a set of poles to lash two canoes together and put a folding table in the space between them. Onto this table we piled all sorts of bundles, and on top of the bundles rode my nephew John, the youngest. As we set out, we came upon two canoeists who looked as if they'd ordered everything, including the canoe, out of the L. L. Bean catalog. We were about a hundred yards apart, but sound carries well over water, so when one of them sniffed and said, "Look at that, Mary; they brought everything but the kitchen sink," we all heard it very clearly.

John cheerfully replied, "Oh no, Mister, we have that too!" as he waved aloft a plastic sink, complete with air-pressure pump and drain plug.

All that stuff and all those people brought out the Type A characteristics in me. I spent the evening trying to get organized but failed miserably: as evening and a light rain fell, we piled into the "cabin" tent with stuff strewn all around us. It rained all night and all the next day. By the second night we were cold and wet, and I was constantly complaining that if we'd been better organized, we would be in much better shape. Then the storm turned nasty. Lightning flashed and thunder roared, rain pounded, and a few old trees in the woods fell down, scaring everyone, including Grandpa.

When we finally fell asleep that miserable night, it was on two sides of a stream that flowed the length of the tent and out the doorway. During the night both the rain and the stream stopped, so I moved in front of the door to stretch out. As the sun began peeking through the trees, John woke up and crawled on top of me to look out on what promised to be a fine day. Overcome by the wonder of our survival, he began to pound my back and shout, "Uncle Eric, Uncle Eric—look, look!"

"What is it, John?" I asked with a yawn.

"Uncle Eric," he exclaimed, "we're alive!" Yes, some things are just naturally more important than others. Setting priorities is a tool to help you find those things.

Getting into the habit of using a bias for action creates energy in our lives. That energy not only gives us greater satisfaction with where we are and where we're going; it also sustains us when the going gets rough.

Pain happens to everyone. In fact, pain may be a central force in keeping us alive and teaching us about life. Think about it: without your sense of pain, you could put your hand in a fire and never feel a thing until the fire had destroyed your hand. Without a sense of pain you wouldn't know to go to the dentist or doctor to have a problem fixed before it became life-threatening.

Pain in our spirit likewise warns us of any spiritual problems we might have and causes us to seek help and initiate change. When a loved one is lost to us through death, grieving is the natural result. From Joy, who's a nurse, I know that grief is a process made up of predictable stages—numbness and anger, for example—some of which are very painful. When we're experiencing grief, we may need the professional help of a clergyperson or counselor.

However, through this painful process called grief we heal. People never become the same as they were before the loved one was lost, but they can become whole again. There may be scars, but they only show where pain has been; they aren't themselves a constant source of pain. Remember pain has one great purpose, it prompts us to take action, thereby avoiding further injury and promoting healing.

One result of the accident I had when I was twenty-one—the accident that revealed to me the strength of Joy's love—was extremely impaired function in my right hand. Since I was right-handed and in school to become a journalist, this was pretty serious stuff to me. I remember the first day in therapy, when the therapist tried to get me to lift a one-gram weight by pinching my forefinger to my thumb. Try as I would—until my hand and arm shook—I couldn't generate enough force to hold one gram. Being a very mature American male, I did the logical thing: I ranted and raved and refused to try anymore. Faced with the stark evidence of my weakness, I preferred to go through life crippled rather than face that weakness over and over. At that moment inaction would have lost me the use of a hand. Fortunately my therapist was a mature American female who knew all the right strings to pull to shame me into giving it "one more try." But the process was painful and long. Two weeks went by before I could lift that one-gram weight. Two months went by before I could lift it with my thumb and little finger. But today I can lift forty or so pounds with that hand, and even though numb on its outer edge, my little finger is doing its part to type these words.

Problems cause us to grow, or, as Chancellor Sweeting put it, "Pressure produces." We used to sit in chapel and say, "Yeah, pressure produces fractures, heartburn, and ulcers." However,

Dr. Sweeting meant it more in the way that pressure on coal produces diamonds. Dr. Peale would tell people who wanted to be rid of all their problems that he could take them to a place where thousands of people had gathered and where there were absolutely no problems—Woodlawn Cemetery in Brooklyn.

Key Discoveries

Preparation

This final chapter in our discussion of the tools for making life work has covered the tools for action. Action is the application of energy to the ideas that give definition to our dreams. We must organize for action by setting goals and then pursuing those goals according to a set of priorities.

These crucial tools are helpful not only to achieve but also to survive the problems that life throws at us. Rather than waste energy shouting and moaning about the problems, we can organize that energy into solutions for the pain. Pain keeps us alive.

Action

Go back to Chapter 6 and the appropriate section of this chapter and reread the practical steps for writing SMART goals and setting priorities. Then do three more practical things:

1. Find a single place to keep a record of your thoughts and writings in this area. For me it's a three-ring binder. For my kids it will be a computer file on c-drive, backed up on a disk. Whether you use file folders, legal pads, steno notebooks, tape recordings, or hieroglyphics, keep your thoughts in one place. Someday that collection of thoughts will come in handy, and today it will give you a physical feeling of progress.

2. Reward yourself when you accomplish a step in the goal-setting process or in establishing priorities. I wrote this book four pages at a time. At the end of four pages I could get up, stretch, and have a cup of coffee and maybe a cookie. When a chapter was finished I could watch a baseball or basketball game. Believe me, those rewards helped me finish.

3. Use the other tools in Chapters 10 and 11 to help in the goal-setting and priority-fixing processes. This book builds principles from front to back. Just as your spiritual framework supports the external parts of your life pyramid, the previous tools of thought-conditioning and imaging can help you with goals and priorities.

PART FOUR

Anchoring Your Life Pyramid, or Let's Talk in the Parking Lot

Most of what I wanted to tell you in this book was concluded in the last chapter. You can get started now on building and strengthening your life pyramid, or—if you choose—you can come into the parking lot for one last discussion.

I'm referring to the high school speaking engagement I mentioned in Chapter 1. You'll remember that I told the nervous superintendent and the students gathered for that speech that we could and would talk about spirituality and God but that if any of them wanted to talk about my religion, we had to wait until after class and go out into the parking lot.

The last subject to cover on this matter of maximizing your spiritual potential has to do with anchoring your life pyramid. Since how I feel about that subject gets awfully close to what most folks call religion, we have to go to the parking lot. You're welcome to join me if you like. I promise it won't be preachy, though it'll be thought-provoking and, depending on your response, perhaps life-changing. But if you want to close the book now and start working on what we've already learned, that will work too—for a while.

By now you're thoroughly familiar with the three-dimensional life pyramid diagram we've been using. While writing this book, I actually made myself a pyramid out of four-inch coffee stirrers. Just a little hot glue at the corners, and there was a not-bad representation of the diagram! The foundation of Belief, Optimism, and Kindness reached up along the framework of Faith, Hope, and Love until they were joined at the spiritual focus on top. Even before the pyramid was built, it wasn't hard to imagine the outward planes of mental, emotional, and physical being filling in the vertical spaces. However, until I made the model, there was one aspect of the pyramid that had eluded me: as I turned my coffee-stirrer pyramid in my hands, examining each surface, I noticed that it actually had *four* sides (if you include the bottom). While I had left that bottom plane blank in my diagrams—the perimeter marked by Belief, Optimism, and Kindness—the foundation of my actual life is anchored in my relationship to God.

After thinking about it for a while, it came to me that this is a perfect illustration of a universal truth about our existence. None of us is alone. We all need to be connected—anchored—to something. This is the reason ancient men and women looked up at the stars and wondered if that was where they had come from. It's the reason philosophers and college sophomores ponder the meaning of life. Inside each one of us is an innate sense that we're a part of something bigger, something universal. There's a longing to be connected to whatever it is that we sense would give greater meaning to our lives. The great American spiritual teacher Billy Graham calls this "the God-shaped vacuum within each human individual."

See, I told you this discussion was going to walk the edge of religion. But before it gets too theoretical and philosophical, let me tell you, as a fellow seeker, how I first felt this vacuum.

Since for most of my life I had grown up with strong and good spiritual teaching, these cosmic questions didn't often intrude into my thoughts. Not many of life's traumas had happened to me, so I was probably a bit smug. Then in the early 1980s my family moved to Glen Ellyn, Illinois. Our three children were all in the toddler stage or beyond, and we were able to buy a little starter home in a great neighborhood surrounded by other families with young children. Next door lived a young couple. Let's call them Mike and Jeanne. Mike was a deputy sheriff, and I have to say it was kind of nice knowing that a lawman lived next door. We did the usual neighborly things: clipping our mutual hedge, shoveling out each other's wives during snowstorms when one or the other of us was away, and mowing the lawn. I never knew Mike well—our families occasionally shared hamburgers on summer evenings, that sort of thing—but when we heard Jeanne was pregnant with their first child, we shared in the rejoicing. They were so happy and excited. With three boys Joy and I were experts, of course, so we were consulted at each point along the way.

Everything went fine for several months, and then Jeanne began to feel unwell. Complications set in, and she was confined to bed for the last weeks of the pregnancy. One morning we heard Mike roar out of the driveway at about 4:00 A.M. and figured the baby had finally arrived. Joy called me at work that day with the sad news that the baby had indeed come, but it had been stillborn.

After I got home from work that evening, I sat on the back deck to sip a soda. When Mike burst through the hedge, I could see right away that something was wrong: his face was flushed, his eyes were bloodshot and wild, and he was unsteady on his feet. In one hand was a bottle of something a lot stronger than his usual light beer. His other hand was out of sight behind his hip.

"Okay, Preach," he called out loudly, "you tell me what God is doing. Why did he kill my baby? *Why did he kill my baby?*" With that Mike threw down the bottle and brought his other hand up, waving his .457 Magnum service revolver. For me, at that moment the world stopped and fear choked me.

"Mike," I croaked, "I'm so sorry for what happened, but please put down the gun. You'll scare Joy and the boys."

"What about you, Preacher Man?" he sneered. "Am I gonna scare you?"

"I'm already scared spitless, Mike," I said. "Please put down the gun."

"Not until you tell me why in the hell God had to kill my baby!" he shouted.

"I don't know what to say, Mike. God didn't kill your baby, but I can't explain why he let it happen."

"What do you mean, you can't explain it," he continued. "You go off to church every week, Sunday after Sunday. Why do you go if you can't explain it?"

"Mike," I replied, "there has to be an answer; all I'm saying is that I don't *know* the answer. Please put the gun down, and we'll talk about it."

"Quit worrying about the gun," he screamed. "It's not for you!" Mike raised the gun to his head and pressed it against his temple. "I just have to know," he sobbed, "where was God when my baby was dying?"

With all my training, with all my upbringing, for several long moments I had nothing to say. Finally, and very feebly, with tears streaming down my own cheeks, I said quietly, "Mike, I do know where God was when your baby died; he was right where he was when his own Son died."

Through his bleary eyes Mike looked at me for a long while. Then he lowered the gun, said "Aw, sh__," and walked slowly through the hedge back home.

I'd like to tell you that I ran after him and we had a long, life-changing talk, but we didn't. I saw little of Mike over the next year, and then we moved away. But Mike has haunted me for twelve years. Mike's life pyramid was being blown apart, and I didn't have the words to tell him how to anchor it. My life—and this book—has been an attempt to help hurting people like Mike find an answer to their search for God. So far my journey has given three answers that may help you:

1. Pain happens, at some time, to everyone. None of us avoids tragedy and difficulty. God doesn't keep us from pain; indeed, the pain we suffer often drives us closer to God.
2. We don't always have the resources to fix ourselves. Sometimes when we want to "pull ourselves up by the bootstraps," we reach down and find that we have no boots, let alone straps. We can't reach God through our efforts even at the best of times. We have to rely on God reaching out to us.
3. The best, most reasonable story I've ever heard of God reaching out to us is the story of Jesus.

To close this part of our journey, let me share how Norman Vincent Peale put this third conclusion at the end of his book *The Positive Power of Imaging:*

> *The last and most important suggestion I have to make is simply this: Stay close to Jesus always. Commit your life to him. He was the first to teach the power that you have within you. He told his disciples, quite plainly, that what they pictured with faith would come to pass. Now, after more than nineteen centuries, scientists and psychiatrists and psychologists are at last beginning to proclaim what the faithful knew all along: He was right.*
>
> *Christ does not change; he is the same yesterday and today and forever. And the truth of his teaching doesn't change either. You can count on it, indeed. You can stake your life on it.*
>
> *The most wonderful thing that can happen to any of us is to have that most profound of all experiences—to know Jesus Christ personally. You can hear about Him all your life and never really know Him. You can believe that He lived and respect Him and honor Him as a great historical figure and still only know Him academically. But when at last you find Him and experience His reality, then for you He comes out of the stained-glass windows and out of history and becomes your personal Savior, then you can walk through all manner of darkness and pain and trouble and be unafraid.*

When we started this book together, I described myself as a Christ-follower on a spiritual journey. Christ is the source of spiritual power in my life, and that power is the anchor for my life pyramid. The apostle John said it best when he wrote, "Yet to all who received him, to those who believed in his name, he gave the right to become Children of God" (John 1:12).

The last word on this book came from my middle son, Nathan. He read most of it in draft form and then said to me, "Dad, this is pretty simple stuff. Are you sure it works?"

My reply? "Just do it."

Afterword

To receive a free copy of Dr. Peale's booklet *Thought Conditioners* or the condensed edition of *The Power of Positive Thinking,* or to obtain a list of his books and tapes available for purchase, write to the Peale Center for Christian Living at the following address:

Box PB
66 East Main Street
Pawling, NY 12564

In addition to works by Norman Vincent Peale, the following books are quoted in these pages: *Love, Medicine, and Miracles,* by Bernie Siegel; and *A Bed by the Window,* by M. Scott Peck. For additional reading, I recommend *Mere Christianity,* by C. S. Lewis; *A Song for Sarah,* by Paula D'Arcy; *A Gentle Thunder,* by Max Lucado; and *Laugh Again,* by Charles Swindoll.

